Supported 4.99

Whitewater Rafting

Whitewater Rafting

Graeme Addison

First published in 2000 by
New Holland Publishers Ltd
London • Cape Town • Sydney • Auckland

US edition published by Stackpole Books

All inquiries should be addressed to:
Stackpole Books
5067 Ritter Road, Mechanicsburg, PA 17055.

2 4 6 8 10 9 7 5 3 1
First edition

ISBN 0-8117-2998-2

Publisher: Mariëlle Renssen
Commissioning Editor: Claudia dos Santos
Editor: Lauren Copley
Designer: Sonia van Essen
Illustrator: Steven Felmore

UK Consultant: Jon Christian

Reproduction by Hirt & Carter (Cape) Pty Ltd
Printed and bound in Singapore by Craft Print (Pte) Ltd

Library of Congress Cataloging-in-Publication Data

Addison Graeme.
    Whitewater rafting/Graeme Addison.—US ed.
    p.cm
  Includes index.
  ISBN 0-8117-2998-2 (pbk)
    1. Rafting (Sports) I.Title.

GV780 A33 2001
796.1'21—dc21   00-061202

Disclaimer

This is a handbook on rafting skills but it is not
substitute for practical training and mentoring b
experienced river-runners.

Although the author and publishers have mad
every effort to ensure that the information con
tained in this book was accurate at the time o
going to press, they accept no responsibility fo
any accident, loss or inconvenience sustained b
any person using this book or the advice given in it

Author's acknowledgements

Brian Joubert tirelessly researched and provided me with expert knowledge of rafting and river conservation in Canada and Southern Africa. Corran Addison, my son, now a top riverboat designer based in Montreal, has taught me more about rivers and technique than anyone else.

Thanks also to the members of the rafting fraternity worldwide who have either contributed to my knowledge of river-running, read the manuscript, or given information via well-kept services on the Internet. They include Hugh du Preez, Andrew Kellett, Steve Camp, Ross Turner, Steve Nomchong, Sue Liell-Cock, Tony Hansen, Billy Edwards, Waldo Van Schalkwyk, Wynand Uys, Jerome Truran, Vladimir Gavrilov, Youry Nemirovsky, Dave Manby, Peter Knowles, Martin Wong, Stan Ricketts, the late David Hall and Lori Pottinger.

To Karen Addison, my wife, thanks for urging me to keep paddling away at the keyboard.

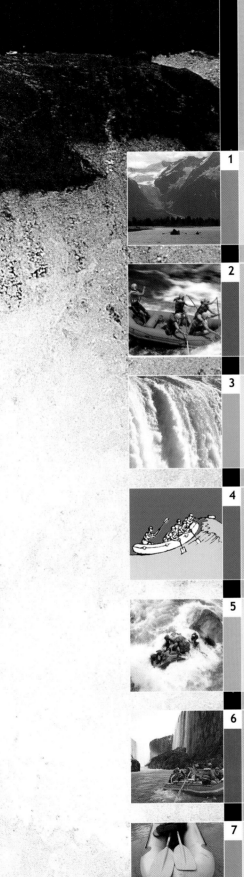

Contents

Spirit of the River

'It doesn't matter what you came to the river for; you'll find out once you get there.'
— Dashka Slater (*'The Use of Rivers'*, in Sierra Magazine)

the raft swings slowly into the current, passengers crouching wide-eyed near the bow. The left oar-blade dips in, making little whorls that spiral away into the river; the right hangs dripping over the water. The raftmaster, who knows this rapid in the Batoka Gorge in Zambezi, Southern Africa, well, grins and heaves on the left blade to pivot the raft so he faces downstream.

The smooth tongue of the rapid slides towards a giant wave that somehow, at close range, seems silent. The black cliffs speed past in the heat of the African sun. Heading directly into the wave, the raft seems suspended in liquid space.

The raft's occupants scream, the oarsman roars his delight, and the inflatable ploughs deep into the foam pile of the breaking wave. The sudden impact is like a freight train striking a heap of wool bales carelessly tossed across the tracks. The raft jolts, sending bits of foam flying.

'High-side!' yells the oarsman, and everyone throws their weight to the side that is tilting ominously. A pile of bodies lurches left, using their weight to avert a capsize. One oar is high in the air, the other deep in the current; the oarsman struggles to keep his balance and as the raft suddenly buckles over the crest, he is pitched into the maelstrom.

No one realizes he is gone. The raft bounces over diminishing waves until suddenly a strong counter-current catches the bow and spins it out of the flow into an eddy behind a boulder. The passengers fall back laughing with nervous relief.

'Hey, where's Sydney?' shouts one, and all look for their missing skipper. 'Thanks for your concern,' comes a voice from the stern where Sydney, the oarsman, is clinging onto the handline strung around the boat. He has ridden the rapid in the wake and now hauls himself on board. As they continue their journey, Sydney, a member of the Ndebele people who live near Bulawayo in Zimbabwe's flat bushland, smiles to himself. For a professional raft guide, this is just another day at the office.

For many thousands of others throughout the world, whitewater rafting represents an exciting break from daily routine. It is an adventure in the wilderness, taking participants to places that can only be reached by highways of water.

If you are fascinated by rivers — by the call to find what lies around the next bend of moving water — then study their wiles. Learn to raft with a technical approach and then you can get yourself down rivers, satisfyingly and safely.

Rafting past and present

Whitewater rafting is one of the leading forms of activity holiday in the world. There is a growing trend towards self-guided whitewater trips, as individuals learn the skills of rafting for themselves.

This opens the way for new personal challenges in the outdoors. It also means that boaters are exploring rivers in more remote areas of the world. The rafting boom has both inward and outward aspects: it penetrates the inner, experiential reality of those who take on the challenge of running rivers; and outwardly it broadens the base of river-running by discovering new raftable rivers in places like Russia and Africa where rivers have not been run for sport until recently.

opposite page TUTEA'S FALLS ON THE OKERE RIVER ON THE NORTH ISLAND OF NEW ZEALAND OFFER AN EXHILARATING EXPERIENCE.

PRIMITIVE RAFTS ARE MADE OF REEDS OR LOGS TIED TOGETHER, AND ARE USUALLY POLED ALONG BY A STANDING CREW.

A MODERN INFLATABLE PADDLE-RAFT REQUIRES TEAMWORK UNDER A SKIPPER WHO STEERS FROM THE STERN (TOP LEFT). THIS IS ONLY ONE OF THE VARIETIES OF MODERN RAFTS.

A popular activity

Most countries have not yet collected statistics on adventure travel because this form of mass tourism is relatively new. However, according to a survey conducted by the Travel Industry Association of America, whitewater rafting is rated the most popular 'hard' adventure sport amongst Americans themselves.

Hard sports entail a marked element of personal physical challenge. Although vastly outnumbered by 'soft' adventurers, who prefer activities such as fishing and hiking, the numbers of hard sports enthusiasts and participants are growing rapidly.

Rafting for fun

Whitewater rafting is a risky business for river guides and the operators, but to the general public, having fun on the water is the key word.

Previously, rivers were seen as obstacles to be crossed or as transport routes for barges and steamers.

Nowadays, the most prized rivers are those that tumble out of the mountains or pour through canyons.

Whitewater is likely to be white only in the higher reaches of rivers. Lower down, silt-load and vegetable dyes leaching into the water turn it brown or brandy-coloured. It is known as 'whitewater' all the same, provided it features rapids.

Origins of today's rafts

The humble raft — probably the earliest form of man's transportation on water — has become a craft with a glamorous adventure image.

Rafts were originally the simplest type of water-craft, used by most cultures, and made up of several logs, planks or reeds fastened together to make a buoyant platform.

The main similarity between rafts of the past and of the present is that they are both relatively light, as they sit on the water rather than drawing a deep draft.

This allows the whitewater inflatable to slip over shallow rocks and bounce off obstacles.

In skilled hands, the modern inflatable raft is able to cross violent currents in rocky rivers and negotiate rapids with style.

Inflatables were developed originally as life rafts and later used by the military for beach assaults. Following World War II, a flood of military surplus inflatables hit the American market. Though these first neoprene rafts were heavy and unwieldy, they quickly became popular with recreational rafters for local river explorations.

By the 1960s, rafting was well established on routes like the Grand Canyon. Demand accelerated the development of new raft designs and materials. In the 1980s self-bailing floors (to let the water out when the raft fills in a rapid) made rafts more manoeuvrable. Rowing frames, packing nets and waterproof boxes and bags turned rafts into supply ships for river passages.

A new breed of rafter emerged, pushing the limits of what was considered possible. In the European Alps, New Zealand's Southern Alps, the South American Andes and Asia's Himalayas, daring kayakers led the way by tackling rivers that no-one thought raftable.

As rafting skills improved and the inflatables themselves became hardier and more manoeuvrable, so commercial raft touring took off all over the world. By the mid-1980s, rivers in South and Central America and Southern Africa were being added to the lists of the world's fun whitewater rivers.

Choices

The 1990s saw three novel changes. The first was the trend towards self-paddled boats, including single-seater oarboats and inflatable kayaks. Rafts were available for hire or sale and any person or group could run downriver without a guide.

This brought about the second change. A spate of accidents led to some official regulation of rafting. Lawsuits emphasizing the responsibilities of river guides, boat hirers and manufacturers have caused companies to be a lot more careful. Anyone undertaking a trip is likely to have to sign a legal waiver of rights, agreeing to the trip at own risk. Cover for whitewater rafting is only offered by *some* personal insurers, so it is important to read both small print and the travel policy brochure.

The third trend has been towards far wider choices in a hugely diversified rafting scene. Trips for children, teenagers, the elderly; corporate team-building tours; women-only, gay and lesbian outings; and rafting for the disabled have all emerged as viable options.

Unfortunately the mass transit business of modern rafting has turned some rivers into Disneylands. The once solitary experience of paddling into the unknown has become relatively rare as thousands throng to do the popular pay-and-go whitewater runs which can be as short as 45 minutes.

Explorations

Fortunately there are still numerous unrun rivers, many of them too dangerous to be rafted even using current technology and skills — though their time may come. Great river explorations continue. Some are too extraordinary to imagine fully, such as the first solo descent of the Amazon from source-to-sea using a hydrospeed (a kind of river toboggan that you push along while swimming).

THE SPORT IS FOR EVERYONE — FROM TEENAGERS TO OLDIES — AND IT HAS CAUGHT ON WHEREVER WHITEWATER RIVERS RUN.

Types of trips

No two river trips are ever the same because rivers themselves change as the water levels vary. At the same time, there are marked differences between various types of trips.

■ Day trips: Many outings only last a few hours and are close to roads and help.

■ Multiday trips: The group runs downriver, stopping overnight, usually to camp out in less accessible spots.

■ Expeditions: This involves a multiday trip into remote country where the group has to be largely self-reliant.

■ Exploration: An expedition down an unknown river is a high-risk undertaking.

Before deciding, consider the following:

■ What kind of trip do you want: easy, moderate, big rapids or extreme?

■ How proficient are the leaders and your companions as boaters?

■ Can you estimate the margins of risk and safety, given your knowledge of rivers?

AT THE PUT-IN, OR LAUNCH POINT ON A RIVER, BOATERS GET READY FOR THE WHITEWATER AHEAD. EQUIPMENT AND PEOPLE ARE COUNTED, LOADS MADE SECURE, AND THE TRIP LEADER GIVES A SAFETY TALK BEFORE THE PARTY SETS OFF.

Rivers in remote places are harder to get to, but are worth the effort. In the mountains around Lake Baikal, on the Siberian side of the Himalayan massif, Russian rafters have pioneered the rivers and offer their 'consulting' guiding services to anyone who has equipment and US dollars.

More than 2400 years ago, Herodotus remarked on the 'vast number' of rafts on the Nile. Nowadays tens of thousands ply the world's rapid rivers, on rafts more sophisticated in design, but still basically floating platforms like their predecessors.

Operators and private tripping

Many people opt for scheduled trips because they want experts to lead them using the right equipment. To put a fully fledged rafting outfit on the water, with all boats and gear, as well as provide transport backup, is expensive to do.

Consider your personal objectives and the possible alternatives, ranging from club trips to ones that are privately organized.

Obviously, these formats affect almost every aspect of trip planning. As far as boating is concerned, the risk rises steadily the further one gets from transport and communications. No two river trips are ever the same because rivers themselves change as the water levels vary. Even a day trip can be dangerous if you enter a wild gorge under the wrong leadership and your personal boating skills and experience are limited.

There will always be a choice between operator-run guided trips and do-it-yourself private or club trips.

As the level of risk increases, so the boating proficiency of the leadership must rise too. One does not have to be a top-rate boater to go on a river trip up to Grade 3, but one does expect those in charge to be experts and skilled in rescue.

AN OARSWOMAN (FOREGROUND) PUSHES THE OARS IN THE CLASSIC 'PORTEGEE' POSITION FOR DOWNRIVER RAFTING. ALTHOUGH OARBOATS MAY BE STROKED BACKWARDS, LIKE ROWING BOATS ON LONG FLAT STRETCHES, IT IS BEST TO FACE FORWARDS (DOWNRIVER) WHEN RUNNING WHITEWATER.

Some rivers allow a great deal of overlap between easy, moderate and serious rafting (See diagram below). Know your limits — don't undertake rivers beyond your level of ability. Establish the overall level of risk and difficulty of a river route.

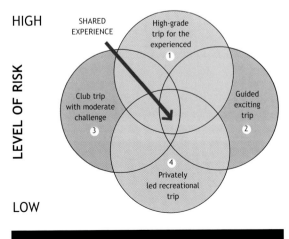

diagram FUN VERSUS LEVEL OF RISK.

1. High-grade rafting: Increasingly, people are running serious rapids on so-called Grade 4 – 5 commercial outings. The general criterion is that one should already have done easier rivers.

2. Guided trip: Many commercial trips fall into this category. Trips range from a few hours to multiday expeditions. The latter demand more of the participants, and reward them with greater personal satisfaction.

3. Club trip: If competently led, the club trip is a good way to learn and meet others who are keen on rafting.

4. Private trips: It is unwise for anyone without much boating or rescue expertise to assemble a trip and hope for the best on the river. Get top amateur or professional leadership if necessary.

Do it Right

'The objective, I believe, is to discover new truths — about our environment, about the peoples we meet, about those with whom we travel, and about ourselves.'
— Richard Bangs *(modern river explorer)*

Why go rafting? A little basic individual and group psychology helps to explain it. People choose rafting as a form of challenge; they take the risks in order to realize something special about themselves. All the more reason, then, to do it right. Select suitable rivers for your level of ability, go with the right companions, have the correct equipment, and adopt the right attitude to safety and your environmental responsibilities.

Whitewater rafting has been described as a 'high risk, low skill' adventure sport. While not strictly true — the risks can be limited by the choice of river, and a lot of skill is involved — there is a grain of truth in the saying. It does not take much for the average person to go rafting, especially if one depends on an established operator to provide skilled guiding and suitable boats.

Privately organized or club trips can go off without a hitch under the right leadership and with the right equipment. It is sheer folly to attack any river without know-how. River-running is 'challenge by choice'.

Basic and higher needs

A complex set of needs drives people to return to their natural habitat, the wilderness. One theory is that people turn to the outdoors to escape the negative stresses of life in industrial society. The outdoors has its own kind of stress (called *eustress*), but it is positive or healthy. Man's evolution as hunter-gatherer has equipped him to cope with eustress. Indeed, people may seek self-fulfilment through exposure to risk.

The idea that 'self-actualization' is achieved through 'peak experiences' comes from the US psychologist Abraham Maslow. He argued that people all have the same basic need for food, shelter, safety, and so on, but that they are motivated by higher needs that he called metaneeds. (Maslow's hierarchy is summarized in the diagram below.)

Rafting fulfils people's metaneeds — our emotional, intellectual and spiritual sides — in various ways. We are moved and fascinated, and a sense of personal peace descends on us as we float along.

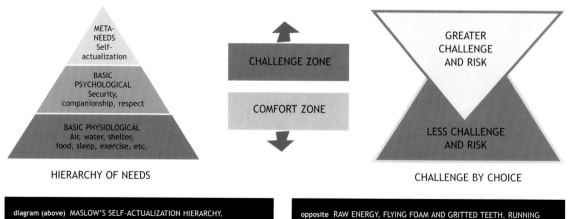

META-NEEDS
Self-actualization

BASIC PSYCHOLOGICAL
Security, companionship, respect

BASIC PHYSIOLOGICAL
Air, water, shelter, food, sleep, exercise, etc.

HIERARCHY OF NEEDS

CHALLENGE ZONE

COMFORT ZONE

GREATER CHALLENGE AND RISK

LESS CHALLENGE AND RISK

CHALLENGE BY CHOICE

diagram (above) MASLOW'S SELF-ACTUALIZATION HIERARCHY.

opposite RAW ENERGY, FLYING FOAM AND GRITTED TEETH. RUNNING WHITEWATER RIVERS DRAWS THRILL SEEKERS EVERY YEAR.

RAFTERS, READY TO GO, LISTEN ATTENTIVELY AS THE TRIP LEADER OUTLINES SAFETY AND ENVIRONMENTAL PRINCIPLES.

levels of risk that allow them to unwind and enjoy the sense of floating through time.

Later we discuss the grading of rivers and offer some thoughts on the complex links between danger and difficulty. To begin with, however, choose rivers that are neither very difficult nor dangerous, but provide the opportunity to learn technique in a nonstressed way. You

More than that, rafting builds human relationships because it involves teamwork. The group is faced with risk and responds positively to eustress by accepting the challenge posed by rapids. Indeed, Maslow's hierarchy is challenged as people find themselves well outside their basic comfort zone. Exposed to the raw forces of nature they pull together for the greater self-actualization of all.

The right rivers for you

Formal training for rafting is available from a number of schools worldwide. As important, if not more so, is 'river time'. Like seasoned old sailors know the oceans in their bones, rafters with river know-how have seen many days on numerous rivers; no course can teach what they know.

Above all, those who know rivers know to ask the question: 'What if?' One may be extremely confident about running a rapid, but what if your raft gets knocked offline and ends up in a horrible mess of rocks? The 'What if?' question focuses attention on the consequences of a mistake. Always ask it.

Choosing where to start is not easy. Rivers range from mere riffles to formidable cataracts from which there is no escape. Although the tendency of the media is to dramatize extreme sports, do not be misled. The majority of river-runners are quite content with lower

Leaders and companions

They say you can choose your friends but never your relatives. Can you choose your companions on the river? Consider these alternatives:

■ A friendly or club trip: the advantage is that you all know each other — or thought you did. Put to the test, friends can show surprising new qualities.

■ A trip organized by an operator (what Americans call an outfitter) takes bookings from all and sundry. Clients like yourself are strangers that you have to learn to get along with.

■ Business associates on a 'team-building' corporate adventure or activity-based conference share a strong motivation to make a success of things.

Mutual dependence is the product of three factors: the leadership, the nature of the challenge and individual abilities and attitudes. Where the three work in harmony, group co-ordination is high; but if they diverge, the group will struggle to cope with the challenge of rafting.

It follows that interpersonal communication and collaborative leadership are the keys to group success on a whitewater trip. Under stress, all groups tend to diverge, so the important thing is to develop team understanding when there is little stress. Talk about things, learn more about each other, and seek a balance between diverse personal qualities. Some people cook well, some raft well, others tell good stories. Mutual appreciation is the bedrock of mutual dependence.

Packing for the river

Packing for the river requires careful planning. Consult outdoor dealers for the latest weather gear, which is constantly improving thanks to research into materials and design.

Manufacturers of river equipment have useful catalogue sites on the Internet, while operators who book trips for clients usually provide a personal kit list. River-runners have three sets of personal gear:

■ 'wet' or on-river gear, including paddling clothes, river sandals or bootees, lifejackets, helmets, and special dry bags for cameras, snacks and extra clothing

■ 'dry' camping and hiking gear, including clothes, shoes, sleeping gear and toiletries

■ travelbag with clean clothing at the back of the shuttle vehicle to change into at the end of the trip

It is wonderful to change out of dripping wetsuits and muddy T-shirts into warm, dry night gear. In many ways, rafters have it easy. Backpackers must hoist and carry everything themselves, and can only take the bare essentials in clothing, equipment and food. In a boat, you can carry many home comforts, including full changes of clothing for the evenings.

Luxurious as it may sound, wet and dry kits are a necessary part of the river experience. Anyone who has spent a night in wet gear after losing a raft with all their kit will agree that one can survive, but the experience is not pleasant.

RIVERS ARE ROUTES INTO THE UNKNOWN, AND DEEP, INACCESSIBLE GORGES — LIKE THIS ONE ON THE GRAND CANYON OF THE YELLOWSTONE RIVER — ALSO SPELL A HEIGHTENED DEGREE OF RISK.

will soon find your level and begin to move up in the ranks of rafting. Remember: paddle within yourself.

Saving our rivers

Throughout this book, a constantly recurring theme is that we are losing our best rivers as a result of dams and environmental destruction. According to a report by the World Commission on Water for the 21st century, backed by the World Bank and the United Nations, more than half the world's 500 major rivers are threatened, seriously depleted or polluted.

The original home of whitewater rafting, the mighty Colorado River in the Grand Canyon, often runs dry near the coast of California. According to the report, it is so exploited that little water is left to protect the ecosystem downstream. The river still thunders through the Canyon itself, though controlled by a major dam. River-runners and environmentalists have taken heart from the policy of decommissioning some dams. But the International Rivers Network, a non-governmental organization campaigning for rivers since 1986, regularly reveals proposals for major dams elsewhere in the world.

One of the best ways to save our rivers is to raft them, get to know them, and promote them as wild and scenic adventure destinations. They are not just there for our sport. Free-flowing rivers constitute the heritage and often the lifeblood of valley communities that have survived over centuries, only to be moved off as modern civilization lays claim to their water.

Know-how and know-not

There is nothing to stop anyone from attempting the most radical river-runs on earth. In theory, anything is runnable. There is even speculation — pursued by astronomers whose hobby is rafting — that when humankind reaches the ice-covered moon of Jupiter, Europa, spacesuit-clad rafters will attempt the channels that may be flowing under the ice.

The difference between a fool on a river and a daredevil with some chance of survival is that the latter has done river time. He or she can see what a rapid demands of the raft crew. 'Hairboaters' — so-called because they run wild rapids where the spray literally resembles hair streaming off the waves — are those who choose to enter the high-risk stakes knowing full well what they face out there.

Ignorant boaters do not know the technical moves necessary for success. In this case, ignorance is not bliss: it leads directly to tragedy. It sets a bad example, drives up insurance premiums, and dissuades others from entering a highly enjoyable sport in the heart of nature.

Preparedness

All river valleys are prey to sudden changes in weather. A hot and sunny day can suddenly turn blustery and chilly even in a tropical climate, and catch you unawares. In Arctic conditions you may be wearing a drysuit with insulation beneath, but you still need to put on raingear.

Be prepared by rafting with a small bag of extra clothing that is accessible to you during the day. A windproof jacket is essential.

THIS CREW MEMBER WHO HAS FALLEN INTO A RAPID IS LIKELY TO BE EXHAUSTED AND WILL STRUGGLE TO CLIMB ABOARD. HERE FELLOW CREW PULL THE SWIMMER ONBOARD BY GRABBING THE LAPELS OF THE PERSONAL FLOTATION DEVICE AND THEN FALLING BACKWARDS INTO THE RAFT.

A A 'FARMER BROWN' WETSUIT LEAVING THE ARMS AND SHOULDERS FREE IS BEST FOR MODERATELY COOL CLIMATES. B A DRYSUIT WITH SEALED NECK, CUFFS AND ANKLES IS NECESSARY FOR VERY COLD WATER. C A STANDARD ISSUE BUOYANCY AID (PERSONAL FLOTATION DEVICE OR PFD) PROVIDES SUPPORT. D TUBS, BOTTLES AND BUCKETS WITH SEALING O-RINGS IN THE LID KEEP CAMERAS AND FOOD DRY. E HELMETS WITH CLOSE-FITTING PADDING AND CHIN STRAPS PROTECT THE HEAD. F A DRY JACKET OR WINDBREAKER IS NEEDED FOR WET, WINDY CONDITIONS. G DRY BAGS COME IN VARIOUS SHAPES, AND CAN ALSO BE TRANSPARENT. H SANDALS, BOOTEES OR TRAIL SHOES SHOULD HAVE NONSLIP SOLES.

TABLE 1: Personal Kit Sets				
SET	PACKING	COLD CLIMATE PRINCIPLES	WARM CLIMATE PRINCIPLES	BOTH
WET GEAR (On river)	■ Day bag with weatherproof clothing ■ Camera bag	■ Layers of clothing ■ Hood, gloves, socks ■ Wetsuit or drysuit ■ Bootees	■ Clothing for sun protection: limbs, hands, neck and face. ■ Sandals / tennis shoes	■ Raingear / windcheater ■ Broad spectrum waterproof sunscreen lotion ■ Drinking water ■ Sunglasses
DRY KIT (Camp)	■ Dry bags (or sealing buckets) packed on rafts and not accessible during the day	■ Warm camp clothing ■ Woollen cap ■ Dry shoes	■ Tracksuit and cap ■ Swimming costume	■ Tent or tarpaulin ■ Sleeping bag and insulation mat ■ Toiletries ■ Insect repellent ■ Book, travel chess, notebook, pen
DRY KIT (Hikes)	■ Small hiking pack, binoculars	■ Additional fleecy shirt and thick trousers	■ Shirt and trousers	■ Trail shoes and hat
TRAVEL CLOTHING	■ Travel kitbag (left packed, with shuttle vehicle)			■ Clean dry clothes to get into at trip end

Cold conditions

Keeping warm from cold water and keeping wind off wet skin are of paramount importance in combating hypothermia (abnormally low body temperature). Follow the layering guidelines in Table 2.

Several light layers insulate better than one heavy garment. Select clothing with nonchafe seams. If the clothing is too heavy it can make you feel very bulky and restrict essential movement in the river.

Wetsuits and drysuits

■ A wetsuit lets water reach your skin, where it warms up. It is recommended for any paddling outside midsummer in temperate countries, and for all paddling on glacial, snowmelt or high mountain rivers. For mild conditions, a 'farmer John' vest-type top with full legs is suitable.

■ A drysuit seals your body from contact with the water with latex or neoprene sealing gaskets. Thermal undergarments of various weight fleece or polyprop retain warmth.

■ One-piece wet- and drysuits are inconvenient for personal ablutions unless you obtain the type with opening flaps or sew these in yourself.

Wind chill

A semi-dry top or lightweight paddle top (short or long sleeves) over the second layer is essential to reduce wind chill. This should be carried in the day bag.

Upper body, head and neck

Much body heat can be lost through the head and neck, so it is important to keep them warm and covered with a neoprene or polyprop skullcap.

TABLE 2: Layering for Warmth		
LAYERS	**WHERE**	**MATERIALS**
FIRST LAYER	Against the skin	Polyprop underwear, consisting of synthetics or microfleece, to keep moisture away from the skin. This should be worn under a wetsuit or drysuit. In very cold weather, a neoprene or woollen hood is worn under the helmet, and gloves are necessary.
SECOND LAYER	Adding thickness	Pile, fleece or wool. These heavier materials are excellent as a middle layer in cool or wet weather. Wool is a good insulator. Wear a jacket or sweater and trousers made of these materials. These are worn over the drysuit or wetsuit.
THIRD LAYER	Outside covering	Rainwear comprises a jacket and possibly also trousers as protection against spray and rain. Plastic materials tend to feel clammy unless breathable, so it is better to opt for coated nylon like Gore-Tex.
FLOTATION	Personal flotation device (PFD)	This is worn between the second and third layers. The PFD is a further insulator and also protects the body against impact with rocks.

Hands and feet

Various gloves are available for cold hands, from the full mitten to those leaving the fingers free for greater movement and efficiency. Insulating socks are worn with shoes or bootees.

Hot conditions

At the other extreme — in warm or hot conditions — clothing is mainly for sun protection but also to avoid wind chill. A lot of clothing can cause dehydration: remember to take in fluids. On rivers, although you often don't feel thirsty, you may find that you lose large amounts of moisture.

■ **Covering:** Rafters' legs and arms are exposed for many hours in the sun. The face is burnt by direct sunlight and by reflections off the water. Of all the sources of radiation, the sun is the most pervasive.

Wear a long sleeved top or shirt that also covers the neck, and a peak on the helmet (detachable peaks can be velcroed onto the helmet).

■ **Sunscreen:** regular and liberal applications of screening creams with a high Sun Protection Factor (SPF) will build up a filmy 'subscreen', provided the cream is water-resistant. Choose a broad-spectrum sunscreen, which protects against both UVA and UVB rays, with an SPF of 15 or higher. Anything below that is a tanning aid, not a protective barrier. (UVA and UVB rays both cause tanning and sunburn, but UVB also causes wrinkling and ageing of the skin.)

■ To keep cool, wear a cotton shirt and denims. Cotton absorbs water and wet cotton clothing acts as a natural refrigerator due to high speed evaporation. Just watch out if the wind picks up — it may cool you down far too much, even on a hot day.

DRYSUITS AND WARMING JACKETS ARE RECOMMENDED FOR VERY COLD WATER.

WARNINGS

■ Do not use a poncho for raingear: it balloons and drags dangerously when swimming.

■ Do not wear gumboots for paddling, as they may drag you down. Worn in Arctic conditions, they should seal into the pants.

■ In cold conditions, avoid cotton garments which have a cooling effect as it permits rapid evaporation.

■ Do not wear natural down clothing (goose feathers) on the water. Once wet, it compresses, becoming useless for insulation.

Drinking water

■ Get a personal water bottle with a strap for shoulder carrying when hiking. Don't drink unpurified river water.

Cameras

Video recorders and still cameras need careful packing, either in a sealed O-ring watertight case or in a dry bag. **A tip:** wrap the camera first in a chamois with an absorbent dishcloth around the outside. Your hands are usually wet just when you want to take action shots, and the dishcloth allows you to dry them before handling the camera. The chamois keeps dust off and cleans the lens. Stow the camera bag securely but accessibly on the raft, but not where it is likely to be hit by paddles or will take impact in a capsize.

All conditions

Personal flotation device (PFD)

A PFD is a buoyancy aid and not a 'lifejacket', and should not be referred to as one. This is partly for legal reasons. It is also to remind people that if they fall in the water they must swim to save themselves.

■ A lifejacket floats the wearer face-up even if unconscious. Some commercial operators on big-water rivers issue full offshore-style 'Mae West' lifejackets.

■ The PFD keeps one afloat but the flotation is distributed around the body. It does not have a bulky collar and is therefore comfortable to wear all day. It is used on rivers because quick rescue is probable.

■ Make sure yours fits snugly and does not ride up over your head when you swim. The zip and buckles should be plastic, not corrodable metal, and there should be no loose loops or straps that could possibly catch on river obstacles.

■ A pocket on the PFD is useful for small items, as is a pouch for a whistle.

Helmet

A helmet should be shatterproof, not made of soft plastic, and should fit snugly.

Look for the following features:

■ Hard plastic (used for proper whitewater helmet or ice hockey helmets) is better than the pliable plastic of skateboard helmets. Reputable river manufacturers will supply the correct grade of plastic.

■ The most dangerous blows are to the forehead and the back of the neck (cortex). The helmet should be well padded inside and especially in those areas.

■ Check to ensure the strap does not loosen when tugged, or the helmet will ride forward over the nose, obscuring your vision.

■ Face masks (as for motorcycling) are often used by paddlers who tackle extreme rapids.

You are entitled to expect that an operator should supply a good helmet, but do check in advance.

One of the oldest fallacies is that in shallow rivers 'you don't need a helmet' — that is exactly where you do need one! In deeper rivers you may be less likely to hit your head, but in any whitewater it is wisest to wear a good quality helmet.

Footwear

■ **Variety:** there is no standard for river footwear. People turn up in bootees, tennis shoes, trail shoes and sandals. Do, however, make sure the shoes stay on in the water and that you can swim effectively while wearing them.

■ **Nonslip:** newer designs have water-releasing soles for traction on wet rocks, a vital consideration. Beware of slippery rocks, and do not jump from rock to rock, even with reliable shoes. Step across.

■ **Gravel:** be careful to keep sand and gravel out of your shoes, as the grinding effect can cause irritations, abrasions and blisters. Wash off your feet or shoes before stepping into a raft.

■ **Hiking:** have a change of shoes for camping and hiking as wet footgear will cause injuries that soon become infected.

Elbow pads

Inflatable kayakers use elbow and shoulder pads to fend off rocks when they run mountain creeks. If you are one of these crazies, go well padded.

Accessories

River stores will be happy to sell you every must-have gadget. The advice here is to do a trip or two before you select the truly useful items, then get the best, which should be rustproof and durable. There are, however, a few proven winners:

■ **Multipurpose tool:** It can saw, fix buckles and pull thorns. Do not use it for cutting bread.

■ **Convertible lounger seat / fold-up mat:** It cushions the posterior, supports the back, and is the envy of all who must sit on the unyielding ground and lean against trees or rocks.

■ **Spectacles strap:** Contact lenses are a controversial subject because they are easy to lose and they pick up grit. A strap will keep prescriptive spectacles and expensive sungasses with you in the worst of swims.

■ **Clips and lanyards** (cord worn around the neck): to hold hats, sunscreen and other items. Beware of too many lines hanging around your neck, and tuck the tubes under your vest.

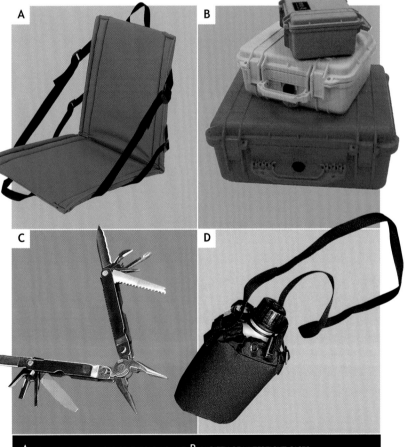

A CONVERTIBLE LOUNGER SEAT/FOLD UP MAT. B VARIETY OF WATERTIGHT CASES.
C MULTIPURPOSE TOOL. D PERSONAL WATER BOTTLE.

The River

every river gets its unique personality from the vegetation, geology, human history and climate of the various regions through which it passes. Less obvious is the fact that the behaviour of all rivers is governed by the same laws of fluid dynamics, making it possible to 'read' the rapids. Experienced rafters should have little difficulty reading the water in any part of the world, since rapids contain very typical features no matter what river you happen to be on.

Fluid dynamics are very complex indeed, so reading the river is not a simple matter. As water levels change from day to day or season to season, so the flow characteristics change too. The river's volume, combined with its gradient (steepness), width, and the rockiness of its bed, determine its rate of flow and the wildness or turbulence of its rapids.

The more turbulent the rapid, the harder it is to predict how a raft will behave. Rivers are fascinating precisely because they are not fully predictable, and no matter how well you know a certain rapid, it can often be full of surprises.

Water flows only downhill, and as a river descends from high to low ground, it forms an upper course, a middle course, and a lower course, each offering different kinds of whitewater experience. A river system will comprise many such watercourses, converging into the main trunk that usually carries the name of the major river — the Colorado, the Nile, and the Yangtze.

■ Tributaries often contain the best whitewater, although rapids are usually found along a watercourse.

■ Steep creeks and cataracts test the limits of a paddler's nerve and technique. Examples abound in the Alps, the Rockies, the Himalayas, the Andes and on the rivers of New Zealand.

■ Mature rivers meander across midland plains where the flow is broad and strong. If the gradient steepens and the underlying rocks are soft, a young river will have cut gorges. With considerable volumes of water in their middle sections, mature rivers provide some of the world's major river-runs. The Colorado River's Grand Canyon is a spectacular example.

■ Finally, rivers reach tidal flats or estuaries that are rich in birdlife. They contain no whitewater except for waves formed by tidal outflows, like those at Skookumchuck off British Columbia, in Canada.

■ Large dams, one of the extensive changes wrought by man, are a mixed blessing for paddlers. Dams impound the water and extensively damage both the upstream and downstream ecology, while irrigation projects, road constructions and factories change the character of the valleys forever. It must be said, though, that timed water releases have fuelled the success of commercial whitewater runs, as on the popular Ocoee River in Tennessee, USA.

Three-way relationship

Rafting involves a three-way relationship between the river, the raft, and the crew. Choosing your raft and handling the boat are dealt with in 'Boat Control'. This chapter concentrates on the river itself, always remembering that it is only one element in the triangle of this relationship.

In theory it is possible to run anything, provided you are confident that you have correctly assessed how all the elements will interact with one another.

opposite page EXPECTANT WHITEWATER RAFTERS TAKE FIRST SIGHT OF THE WHITE NILE, NEAR JINJA, UGANDA.

Naming the parts

By general agreement, River Left (RL) and River Right (RR) are always on your left or right as you look downstream (Diagram 1). The glossary (featured on p 94) names typical features, but the processes at work in every rapid need to be clarified further. One learns best by doing. The main benefit of river-talk and knowing the features of a flowing river is that it can pinpoint what one needs to look out for.

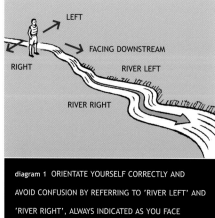

diagram 1 ORIENTATE YOURSELF CORRECTLY AND AVOID CONFUSION BY REFERRING TO 'RIVER LEFT' AND 'RIVER RIGHT', ALWAYS INDICATED AS YOU FACE DOWNSTREAM.

bank, preferably a high point, and make a mental image of it. Recall where the rocks are and what the currents are doing. Have some alternatives in mind so that if the river knocks you offline you can execute some slick boatwork to avert disaster.

The big picture

Everything about reading the river is based on the big picture — assimilating as much information as you can about a rapid before running it. This will guide your actions if you encounter any surprises.

Look and listen

Reading the river is about understanding what the body of the water is doing and thereby making inferences from the visible signs on the surface. To the practised eye, waves and eddies tell a story.

A rapid that is 'smoking' with rising spray is likely to be far more exciting than one that is shunting along without fireworks. The ear can be as important as the eye. A sinister hiss can denote a dangerous 'hydraulic' or 'hole' that may trap and hold a boat, while a loud roaring sound may be nothing more than big waves waiting to welcome you. A hole captures the river's energy in one spot, creating a pounding rotational action as water from downstream pours back upriver.

Four dimensions

Most people will readily acknowledge that a river is three-dimensional — it has length, breadth and volume — yet river-runners also have to reckon with a fourth dimension: time. What happens from moment to moment will determine the outcome of your run down-rapid. One needs to be equally concerned with each stage of the rafting run, not just the beginning.

Scouting the line

The route a boat picks through a rapid is called the 'line'. In preparing your line, look at the rapid from the

Rapid forms

Rapids differ significantly in form depending on what causes them (Diagram 2).

■ **Staircase:** In mountain creeks the channel is as wide as it is deep, descending over drops with little pause (A). Banks may be steep and visibility is poor.

■ **Pool-and-drop:** Most popular rapid-runs take this form. Big rivers are far wider than they are deep, and tend to pool or flow slowly between rapids (B). Rock bands narrow and steepened gradients cause rapids that include hazards such as big drops and hydraulics.

■ **Confluence:** Strong whirlpools and eddies/eddy fences occur where two or more rivers or currents join (C). Thick vegetation is a characteristic of confluence rapids, reducing visibility.

■ **Compression:** Where big water volumes are constricted by river bends or canyon walls, inside bends develop waves, while the current hammers into the outside bend. Domes of water boil up from below (D).

■ **Big water:** This describes high-volume runs that generate powerful forces. Flood conditions cause surges and moving hydraulics. Floods also wash obstacles like trees along, forming moving strainers.

■ **Man-made:** Rapids may be caused or accentuated by the intervention of man (dam outflows, bridges) and especially by wreckage, dump tips and construction rubble. Avoid these obstacles where possible — they consist of sharp rocks, scrap metal and trailing wires, and are usually dangerous.

Wave forms

Wave forms (Diagram 3) differ with gradient and the profile of the riverbed. River waves are quite unlike sea waves. In the sea, the waves move and the water stands still. In the river, the waves stand still while the water moves through them. As sea waves break, they disperse their energy. The energy in river waves is constantly renewed as the water continues pouring down the slope. The result is that river waves maintain their power, and should not be underestimated.

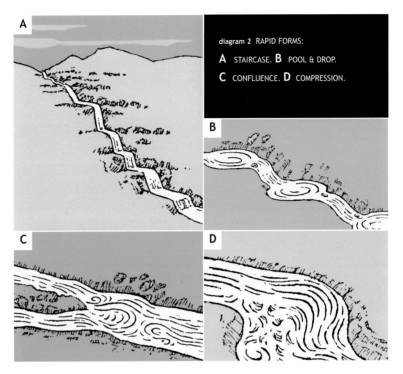

diagram 2 RAPID FORMS:

A STAIRCASE. **B** POOL & DROP.
C CONFLUENCE. **D** COMPRESSION.

Standing waves form 'wave trains' (A) that turn into breaking waves (B). In wilder rapids, they become piles of tossing foam called 'haystacks' (C). Ultimately, as the wave folds over on itself, it becomes a foam pile (D). In all these wave forms, the powerful force of the water is flushing through and will carry boats and swimmers on downriver.

It takes a rock or ledge under the water to form a hole, or 'hydraulic' with a strong suck-back action (E). Holes, which are often highly aerated, are also known as reversals. Floating objects tend not to be very buoyant in this aerated water and may remain under the surface. A log, a boat or a person caught in a reversal may be perpetually churned around in this hole slot, which is known as a 'keeper.'

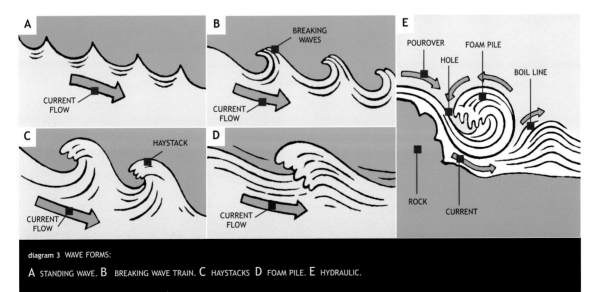

diagram 3 WAVE FORMS:

A STANDING WAVE. **B** BREAKING WAVE TRAIN. **C** HAYSTACKS **D** FOAM PILE. **E** HYDRAULIC.

Features and hazards of rapids

The river is a dynamic medium, so when its features are described in static terms, don't forget that they are moving with constantly renewed energy.

Vee or tongue

The tongue, or smooth V-shaped surface of the current as it enters the top of a rapid, indicates a deep channel that leads into a wave train. On the tongue you have a brief respite or 'quiet time' to brace for the action to come.

Lateral wave

Waves coming off the bank or midstream obstacles at an angle are called laterals. They can flip a raft and large ones should be met head-on.

Eddy

An eddy is a mild to powerful swirl forming behind an obstacle. Eddies are assets to river-runners as boats can park in them. Boiling eddies are very unstable and are not really suitable for parking.

EXTREMELY DANGEROUS WHIRLPOOLS ARE RARE ON MOST RIVERS. HOWEVER, THE EYE OF THIS WHIRLPOOL (RED SQUARE) COULD BE POTENTIALLY FATAL. THE SCALE IS SHOWN BY THE WOMAN ON THE ROCKS (ENCIRCLED IN RED).

Eddy fence

The line of friction between the upstream eddy and main current is the 'fence', where volumes of water rub together creating a zone of turbulence, or vertical shear where both up-and-down currents occur. Sometimes the eddy fence stands up like a barrier that has to be crossed with determined paddling.

Whirlpool

Where the river suddenly widens after a narrow section, a recirculating whirlpool may form in the deep open backwater, with a vortex sucking down near the middle. Always swim with your back to the vortex, often called the 'eye', to escape the pull.

Cushion

When the current piles up against a rock, cliff-face or other obstruction, the resulting cushion prevents boats from hitting the obstacle too hard. However, it can be big enough to flip a raft.

Pourover

Current that pours over rocks can form a hole behind them, known as a pourover. Seen from upstream, a pourover looks like a hump in the water with whiskers of whitewater on both sides. Skirt it, but if you do go over the top, paddle hard to jump the hole slot that forms immediately below the rock.

Hole or hydraulic

This reversal in the flow is potentially dangerous, although safe holes are suitable for playboating. A sure sign of a hole is the boil line lying downstream, where water from deep down rises and returns upstream.

Holes may be very violent, with no clearly visible boil line — just a foamy current sucking backwards.

Keeper

Keepers are holes with a continual cyclical motion and no easy way out. A keeper may not appear large, but it could hold a boat and swimmers for a long time if there is a clear boil line below the pourover. Keepers may pull back very powerfully, so rescue may be essential.

Weir or low-head dam

A wall built across the width of the river creates a deep aerated slot below. Weir action is symmetrical, creating a keeper hydraulic from which it may be nearly impossible to paddle or swim out. Weirs are known killers. Do not run them.

Boulder garden

Large boulders break the river into a multitude of channels in which visibility is usually poor. At higher levels, the rocks may create a section littered with holes and pourovers. Boats can wrap on the rocks.

Siphon and undercut

When the current is channelled through potholes and piles of boulders, it often forms undercut ledges or pipes that suck down in true siphon action. Always give boulder 'sieves' a wide berth.

Strainer

Tree roots or branches, piled flood debris, wire mesh or industrial scrap will literally keep boats and swimmers back like tea leaves in a strainer. Climb up onto the strainer immediately to avoid getting pulled under the water.

around 1.9m per km (roughly 10ft per mile). But the Colorado is a pool-and-drop river, with stretches of flat water broken by rapids. Some of its rapids have a gradient of 35ft per mile, making up for the lack of gradient on the long pools.

■ **Mild rapids** are likely on rivers with less than 5ft per mile gradient.

■ **Moderate rapids** are to be expected up to 35ft per mile.

■ **Serious rapids** with waterfalls or cataracts are likely over a constant gradient of 35 – 200ft per mile.

To estimate the gradient, look at a topographical map with the contours marked. Where successive contours cross the river, measure the distance between them along the riverbed. A map wheel can be used or a piece of string can be laid on the map following the river's course. The gradient is the height of the contour in proportion to the riverbed distance.

COURSE PARTICIPANTS IN A SWIFTWATER RESCUE CLASS PRACTISE HOW TO EXTRICATE A SWIMMER WHO HAS BECOME TRAPPED IN A STRAINER.

Gradient

Gradient is an important measure of the river's likely level of difficulty. River-runners conventionally use 'feet per mile' to describe gradient, because 'metres per kilometre' gives a less exact picture. The gradient of the Colorado River in the Grand Canyon is, overall,

Mechanics of flow

Fluid such as water runs along a channel in a simple laminar or layered flow (see Diagram 1 on p 30) provided there are no obstacles or sudden changes in gradient. The fastest current in a river flows in the

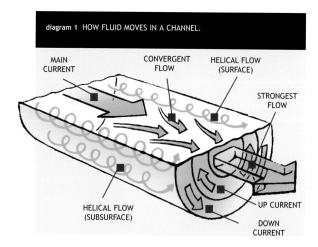

diagram 1 HOW FLUID MOVES IN A CHANNEL.

MAIN CURRENT

CONVERGENT FLOW

HELICAL FLOW (SURFACE)

STRONGEST FLOW

HELICAL FLOW (SUBSURFACE)

UP CURRENT

DOWN CURRENT

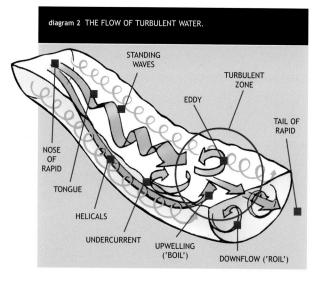

diagram 2 THE FLOW OF TURBULENT WATER.

STANDING WAVES

TURBULENT ZONE

EDDY

TAIL OF RAPID

NOSE OF RAPID

TONGUE

HELICALS

UNDERCURRENT

UPWELLING ('BOIL')

DOWNFLOW ('ROIL')

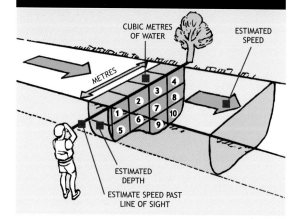

diagram 3 ESTIMATE THE FLOW BY GUESSING SPEED AND DEPTH. CUBIC METRES X SPEED PER SECOND = CUBIC METRES PER SECOND (CUMECS). THIS FLOW IS ROUGHLY 10 CUMECS, IF SPEED IS ONE METRE PER SECOND.

CUBIC METRES OF WATER

ESTIMATED SPEED

METRES

ESTIMATED DEPTH

ESTIMATE SPEED PAST LINE OF SIGHT

centre of the channel — just beneath the surface — as friction with the air slows down the top layer. Against the banks, friction sets up spiralling currents technically called helicals. These converge on the main current, so a river's natural tendency is to carry boats and swimmers towards midstream.

Turbulent flow (Diagram 2) tends towards chaos. Even the most powerful modern computers cannot model turbulence in any detail, which makes this diagram just an approximation.

When there is a sudden drop in gradient, standing waves form in the main current. The surface looks like a carpet that has been pushed up into folds. From the top end of the rapid, a smooth 'tongue' leads into the standing waves, which tail off at the end. Since water is heavy, part of the current flows down to the bottom. It forms an undertow, then bounces up as 'boils'. In the zone of maximum turbulence, eddies form as the main current slows and spins, and lateral waves crash in from the sides. Complex as this picture is, it realistically conveys the confusion of currents in a simple rapid. Add some rocks and twists in the channel, and the outcome is wilder.

Estimating flow

The volume of water in a river, measured in cubic metres per second (cumecs) or cubic feet per second (cfs), determines the kind of run you will have. It is sometimes essential to know the water flow in advance, as trips may have to be cancelled due to dry river or flood conditions.

One can usually obtain flow statistics from the local water authority. In developed countries, it is becoming fairly common to find these on the Internet, although it is advisable to check the latest statistics by telephone. In the absence of official figures, contact farmers or local residents for their estimates ('low', 'medium' or 'high').

Experienced rafters or local operators can also predict the kinds of run you will have, given the cumecs or cfs.

On-river, estimate the flow yourself (Diagram 3).

■ Look directly across a channel through which the whole river is flowing.

This innovative river mapping method suggests how to mark the features and hazards of whitewater. Note that maps should be dated and should include the estimated level (low/medium/high) because river features can change markedly.

N
W ✦ E
S

R
L
350m / 383yd

Basil Jones
16 May 2000

- ORIENTATION: River left and right as shown with the current from bottom to top.
- INDICATE rough direction of north
- LENGTH of rapid in metres or yards
- ESTIMATE flow level
- DATE and SIGN the map
- NAME the rapid and river

Advisory

Set up rescue

Scout

Pull-out

Walk

Put-in

River Features

Vee or tongue

Rocks

Moving flatwater

Rapid current

Whirls and boils

Eddy

Haystacks (very wild)

Standing waves

Shoal

Cushion

Lateral wave

River Hazards

Hole

Smiling hole

Frowning hole

Keeper hydraulic (e.g. weir)

Strainer

Siphon

Undercut

Whirlpool

11m

Waterfall and height

A

B

C

A LOW WATER. **B** MEDIUM WATER. **C** HIGH WATER.

■ Try to guess the speed of the water passing between yourself and a marker like a tree opposite, perhaps by throwing a log in and timing its progress.

■ Guess the depth or try to measure it with a pole. From this you can estimate the cubic volume of the river passing you in the channel every second.

River conditions: low to high

Rivers change dramatically as the water levels rise after rain or a dam release.

■ **Low water:** the gradient is steeper and the run can be excitingly technical. Rocks and strainers stick out, the channels are narrow and difficult to negotiate. With less energy in the flow, rapids turn sluggish and you may have to drag or carry the boats.

■ **Medium water:** Because the channels are wider and wilder, this is often the best level. Holes begin to appear as the obstacles are covered, and with more force carrying you downriver faster, anticipation is the key to good navigation.

TABLE 1: RAPID GRADING			
GRADE	**DESCRIPTION**	**DIFFICULTY**	**DANGER**
1	Fast water with waves but no serious obstructions	Very easy	No danger except for the risks posed by moving water
2	Rapid that requires some manoeuvring	Easy, but it may challenge the inexperienced	Somewhat risky if people hit rocks or take swims
3	Big, noisy and complex, with rocks, currents and turns	Not easy, requires nerve and co-ordination. Possible for crews with good skippers	Moderate danger, especially from long swims or pinnings on rocks
4	Wild and powerful water which can be scouted to plan the line, but surprises are likely	Difficult — beyond the competence of the average touring boater	Dangerous to swimmers, and likely to wrap rafts on rocks or keep swimmers in holes
5	Long, violent, unpredictable rapid with multiple channels, drops, holes, and surges. Poor visibility makes scouting risky	Only experts should attempt this type of rapid	Extremely dangerous — injuries and drowning are real possibilities
6	Extreme water that is continuous and offers no routes of escape. Its complexity makes it almost impossible to read	Unrunnable	Likely to be fatal, no matter how good the boater/s
+ 1	To all of the above, add 1 grade for cold water or cold weather, and/or 1 grade for remoteness from help (over two hours from a road or telecommunications). You can try anything if there is no real danger, but always ask 'What if?'		

■ **High water:** The channel is filled bank to bank without overflowing. Hydraulics form everywhere; boats are carried along haphazardly. Because the water is fast and murky it may be difficult to see bad holes ahead or tell the difference between mere standing waves and hydraulics. Swims are likely to be long and exhausting.

■ **Flood:** Unpredictable and extremely dangerous. The river tops its banks and runs into forests and fences creating monster strainers, while smoking rapids and turgid brown water make reading the river almost impossible.

Rapid Grading

Confronted with a rapid, people want to know: 'Can we run it?' This question is usually answered by grading or classifying the rapid from 1 to 6. Grade 1 is easy and safe while Grade 5 is at the limit of expert ability, and Grade 6 is unrunnable.

The 'international scale of river difficulty' has been widely publicized. Although the system is applied worldwide, it remains controversial because it mixes up difficulty (degree of technical boating ability required) and danger (the consequences of a mistake in terms of physical risk). Although the two tend to go hand-in-hand, it is not always so.

For example, an easy run over a waterfall (just go straight) can have serious consequences at the bottom if one gets trapped in the suck-back! Meanwhile, a very difficult rafting route through boulder gardens may pose no serious danger even if rafts capsize and people have to swim.

Table 1 details a two-step system of rapid grading that separates the difficulty (degree of technical boating ability required) from the danger (consequences of a mistake). It is then possible, for instance, to grade a waterfall as a 2 — 5: a 2 for difficulty (easy entry) but a 5 for danger (keeper hole at the bottom).

Within the grades, boaters often talk of a 'low', 'medium' or 'high' grade, so that a low 4 (4-) is considered easier or less dangerous than a high 4 (4+). Both can be scouted and run by very competent oarsmen or kayakers, and well-skippered paddle rafts.

Table 2

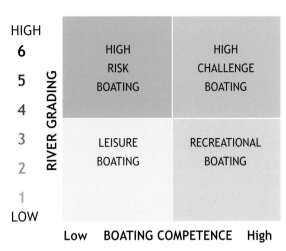

Grading tends to be a subjective matter, and many people may still be concerned about their personal safety despite having discussed the features of a stretch of river.

Table 2 might help to judge whether you will be able to run a rapid or not. Remember that guided trips under competent boaters will reduce the risk and increase the challenge, allowing average boaters to undertake riskier adventures.

■ Take the grade of the rapid and factor in the assumed level of 'boating competence' of the skipper and crew members.

■ Plot the result in the squares to tell you what kind of boating you are about to undertake.

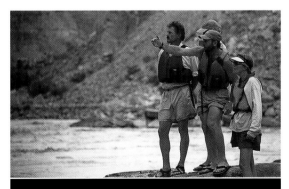

TO SCOUT A RAPID FROM THE BANK, GET OUT AND WALK, DISCUSS, POINT OUT THE HAZARDS, AND CHOOSE YOUR LINE.

Scouting rapids

Few boaters have the privilege of scouting the river from a helicopter, but if you get the chance, go for it. Stopping above the rapid and walking along the bank is the usual way of doing things. A savvy boater stands on a high point and examines the rapid, then tells the group the right line to run. People may agree, dissent or suggest other lines, and often some opt for one line and some for another.

Never feel pressured to run a rapid. Those who are only too keen to get going without enough careful analysis may learn a lesson. Those who are too nervous to hold their paddles but go anyway may have to be rescued later in a state of shock. Know your limits.

What if?

It's important to get a scout's-eye view of the rapid. The scout spots a number of hazards and very wisely asks, 'What if' we get into trouble?

Viewing the rapid

Try to get several views of the rapid (see diagram below). This may not be possible if the banks are sheer or slippery. Wear your helmet and PFD while scouting.

- The view from upstream (A) gives the least information because the rapid is out of sight below the horizon line.
- The view from the middle (B) lays out the whole course, but does not give you much idea of what it will feel like on the water.
- If you view the rapid from below (C), you will have to walk the entire course, which can be a very educative experience.
- Mentally record the lie of the rapid. It is often helpful to draw it in the sand — especially when discussing it in a group — or sketch it in a notebook for reference on later trips.

Codes of safety and ethics

Most clubs, operators and national rafting associations have codes of best practice and right conduct for the river. Codes provide a shorthand way of reminding everyone of their rights and responsibilities in the typical situations that arise on most rivers.

Safety codes

Probably the best-known set of safety rules and advice comes from American Whitewater, a US association with thousands of individual members and hundreds of clubs affiliated to it, and it is obtainable over the Internet (see contacts at the end of this book). Key points of the safety code should be included in the safety talk given prior to setting off.

All codes should stress the following:

- Avoid rivers that exceed your boating competence.
- Wear the correct safety gear (buoyancy aid or life jacket, helmet, sun-and-cold protection and footgear).
- Do not boat alone, and go with leaders who can read the river, are correctly equipped, and have training in rescue skills and first aid.

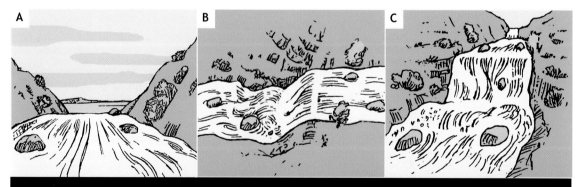

diagram: A RAPID LOOKS VERY DIFFERENT DEPENDING ON WHERE YOU ARE STANDING. IF YOU CANNOT SEE WHAT LIES AHEAD, GET OUT AND SCOUT.
A VIEW FROM UPSTREAM. **B** VIEW FROM A HIGH POINT IN THE MIDDLE. **C** VIEW FROM DOWNSTREAM.

■ Boats and equipment must carry a repair kit and be in working order.

■ Everyone shares responsibility for the trip. They must exercise personal judgement on safety and environmental issues, and show consideration for group members and other river users.

■ Commercial guides or instructors have a legal duty to care for those in the group, but every participant undertakes the trip at his/her own risk.

■ The trip plan should be communicated to all group members and filed with the authorities or a responsible person who will take prompt action if the group is overdue.

■ Anyone may opt to walk around a rapid, if that is possible. Discuss alternatives when scouting.

■ A trip may be terminated due to accidents, flooding, illness or incapacity, but the group must stick together until it reaches safety.

■ The group must carry a full medical kit and emergency supplies with signalling devices.

Rules for high-grade rivers (4 & 5)

More exciting and challenging rivers are being run everywhere, adding to the standard requirements from leaders and the participants.

■ A maximum ratio of 1:8 guides to clients (or experienced leaders to average crew) should apply on rivers over Grade 3, with 1:4 in serious water.

■ Participants should have completed at least one river trip on a Grade 3 river and should be properly informed about the risks to come.

■ Escape and evacuation routes from the river valley should be planned and co-ordinated properly with local rescue services.

Show respect

Beyond safety issues are matters of health and hygiene, respect for others, and protection of the ecology.

■ Access to rivers needs to be negotiated. The necessary permission should be obtained and the rights of landowners respected.

■ Every individual is committed to minimum physical impact on the environment, and leaders will set a personal example. Noise will be kept down, waste will be compacted and carried out with the group. The group will not cut natural vegetation or burn wood indiscriminately.

■ To reduce crowding and improve the quality of the river experience, tripping groups will not all depart simultaneously. They will make an effort to stay apart on the river, especially at rapids that need to be scouted, and at overnight camps.

■ To maintain good relations with local people and indigenous inhabitants, groups will buy local produce, employ helpers from the population where possible and accept cultural practices.

Reduce impact

Ever had the experience of coming across plastic bags, beer cans and cigarette stubs in a hitherto pristine natural environment? Litter should be picked up and taken away because the wildlife may ingest the plastics or cut themselves on glass.

THE TRANQUIL MOOD OF WATER AT SUNRISE AND SUNSET IS PART OF THE ATTRACTION OF RIVER TRIPPING, SO RAFTERS SHOULD ENSURE THAT CAMPSITES ARE LEFT SPOTLESS.

Serious impacts are caused by:

■ hardening of the ground around campsites with multiple fireplaces and pathways. This reduces the ability of the natural vegetation to regenerate and will cause soil erosion;

■ stripping of trees and brush for firewood, which removes ground cover and destroys the micro-habitats of insects, birdlife, reptiles and small mammals;

■ pollution of the landscape and river by human and kitchen waste, solids and liquids, making an area both unhealthy and unsightly. In the river, waste breeds bacteria and interferes with fish feeding cycles.

Some conservation authorities insist on everything being itemized by a group prior to the trip. Spot checks are then conducted during the trip and afterwards.

Voluntary environmental controls are far better in principle. These include:

■ Pack it in, take it away when you leave! This applies to all refuse, packaging and human waste.

■ Use a portable chemical toilet. (It may be unnecessary on long expeditions exploring new rivers, but is necessary everywhere else.)

■ Sweep the kitchen area for food scraps and burn these in the fire. Use a firepan, not the bare ground, and pack out the embers when you leave.

■ Avoid wasteful bonfires and opt for gas cookers where practicable. Use slow-burning logs for small social fires.

■ Dispose of waste water — including dishwater, toothpaste and washing water — in a knee-deep pit, at least 100m (109 yd) above the highwater mark. This is filled in when the group leaves.

■ Keep wildlife wild by avoiding sensitive habitats, and do not introduce new species — especially pet dogs — into a wildlife area.

Sensible campcraft

Many camping impacts can be avoided if the camp itself is sensibly set out. Have a circular flow plan with a kitchen and serving area, a cleaning area, a social area and a waste-handling area out of the way.

Always draw water from a flowing section of the river where people are unlikely to swim or wade around the boats.

Use a three-bucket system for dishwashing: the first with river water to rinse off the plates, the second with warm soapy water to wash them, and the third with disinfected water to clean them before drying. Put scraps in a bag-lined refuse bin for packing out.

Shelter for all seasons

Select campsites where a sudden rise or fall in the river will not seriously affect your safety, and stay out of dry streambeds, which could fill up with flash floods. Think about where the morning sun will strike: you may want warmth in a cold valley. In hot climates, being in shadow for as long as possible may be the best option.

Apart from personal tents, the group may need a shelter in the form of a tarpaulin — sometimes called a 'wing' or 'tarp' — which protects the catering or social areas. It is unwise to use paddles for tent poles because the load can bend or break them. Rig the 'wing' below a bank or trees if the wind is blowing, or it will go flying. Tarpaulins can be used to collect clean rainwater or dew condensation, provided it is clean.

LEARNING TO THROW UP A TARPAULIN SHELTER AT SHORT NOTICE KEEPS OUT LIGHT RAIN AND SNOW AND ALSO ACTS AS AN EFFECTIVE SHADECLOTH AND DEW BARRIER.

Group equipment

River camping equipment is quite highly specialized and it is best to obtain it only from river suppliers, not general camping stores.

Thousands of handy items are shown in mail order or Internet catalogues. To buy them all would bankrupt a non-millionaire, but some things are essential and others really useful for the group.

Essentials

■ Dry boxes to seal in food and keep it cold. A dry box will have an O-ring around the inside rim and should clip or strap closed tightly — enough to stay unopened in a capsize.

■ Roll-up camp tables are extremely functional — they pack away without sharp protruding edges. Small fold-up tables are especially useful for food preparation.

■ Collapsible canvas or PVC buckets for fetching water and washing up can be rolled up and stowed when not in use.

■ Camp chairs comfort the posterior but they are bulky to carry. An alternative is the rigged fold-mat, which doubles as a padded groundmat for sleeping.

■ A kitchen bag for strange-shaped items like kettles and pots is handier than a box, as it pads utensils .

■ Stoves or gas cookers must be carried, for environmental reasons as well as for quick heating of soups and brews on cold days.

Toilet tales

A 'rocketbox' is the familiar name for a portable toilet that must accompany trips on well-used rivers. Smaller groups have smaller needs and can use the 'boombox'.

On operator trips, toilet duties are rotated among guides or among everyone on private trips. The duty becomes a game and a challenge when the person setting up the box seeks the prize-winning lookout point from which to contemplate nature while seated.

Every morning the portable toilet is one of the last items to be loaded on the boats, after the call has been made for 'Last rites!'

Stowing the toilet holds few of the terrors that used to attend these devices when the waste had to be

A FOLD-UP CAMPING TABLE FOR EATING OR FOOD PREPARATION.
B CAMPING GAS COOKER. C HIKING DRY BAG.
D FOLD-UP CAMPING CHAIR. E CATERING BOX FOR PREPARING MEALS.

bagged and carried loose in the boats. Nowadays tightly closed chambers prevent ruptures amid the violence of the river.

For emergency stops along the river, carry a small trowel and make your deposit well above the high-water mark. Burn the paper, do not bury it; it may survive years in a dry climate.

Shuttle diplomacy

Like military expeditions, river trips entail transporting people and equipment over rough terrain. Various procedures need to be planned thoroughly to avoid confusion and considerable annoyance. Especially at the end of the trip, participants do not like to be delayed when they are tired, wet, hungry and keen to clean up and get home.

Vehicles need to be shuttled to drop off the people at the top of the river and collect them at the bottom. Commercial operators use paid drivers. On private trips, operators work out a scheme — diplomatically

IN BETWEEN THE RAPIDS THERE IS ALWAYS TIME TO RELAX ON THE RIVER AND ENJOY THE PEACE OF RIPPLING WATER.

and to the satisfaction of everyone — so that drivers are not left behind or expected to pay for all the fuel. A Trip File containing load details and information about access and times needs to be with the vehicles.

Special points about take-outs:

■ Leave the keys with the vehicles or with a trustworthy person near the vehicles. There could hardly be a worse way to end a trip than finding that the keys are lost or that the immobilizer button has been damaged by water.

■ Drivers must not drink alcohol. Statistically the most dangerous moment of a river trip appears to be the return drive, when people are relaxed and allow themselves to unwind.

■ Be aware of fatigue and sleepiness.

Enriching the experience

The modern movement for experiential education believes that outdoor adventure enriches us by teaching us the evolutionary lessons we have forgotten in the process of becoming urbanized.

Whitewater attracts many for its pure adrenaline rush, but it offers wider rewards, and perhaps some that are more meaningful in the long run. Relaxing next to a swirling current, thinking or reading, is a form of relaxation not given to city dwellers.

River tripping should also be fun. Mud-fights, so long as they involve volunteers only, are inevitable when the weather is warm and the river drops to reveal mud-banks. A favourite on-water pastime, 'Boat-stacking', involves building the highest platform of different boats and piling human pyramids on top.

Interpretative trailing

The most enriching part of whitewater sport is being surrounded by a natural environment which harbours wildlife and may have changed little in appearance since the first explorers followed rivers as routes of discovery. Archaeological evidence of human prehistory is frequently found in caves and on canyon walls in the form of pictographs.

To interpret the outdoors, do not depend on hearsay or guesswork. Here are three suggested ways to improve the quality of your river experience by making use of expert knowledge:

■ **Buy the book:** Bookstores have plenty of excellent guidebooks ranging from travel information to field guides on nature. Read up in advance, make notes and if there is room, take a small library along. Always keep the books and writing materials very dry by wrapping them in cloth and stowing them in a special mini dry bag.

■ **Invite the specialist:** Invite a zoologist, archaeologist or other specialist along to provide trail interpretation. Experts usually identify ecological niches or sites of interest for short interactive talks. If you record what they say, you will have it for the next trip — when an expert in another field may add knowledge of further niches and sites.

■ **Get to know the people:** Only with the co-operation of local people can adventure travel and tourism remain sustainable, and the environment be conserved for wilderness trails. If among foreign people, get a phrasebook or even hire an interpreter. You will learn a good deal about heritage and history if you stop off in villages to make friends. Take care though, over security, as theft and violence can occur the world over.

Bites and frights

Things that crawl and fly, bite and sting, scare you and annoy you, are rife on rivers — naturally so, it is their habitat. Only the flies and scavengers that we bring with us should not be there; as for the rest, we are guests in their territory.

One cannot name all the threats to safety and health posed by nasties in the outdoors. There are still some common denominators covering most parts of the world on which to get prior information and take precautions where possible.

If you are planning to visit a country where you are likely to encounter dangerous wildlife, consult the local authorities for advice.

Watch out for:

■ Parasites that transmit diseases to the blood through contact with water that has been infected (e.g. giardia and bilharzia).

■ Disease-carrying insects, like the anopheles mosquito, which carries malaria.

■ Dangerous spiders and snakes which may be endemic to the river valley in which you find yourself. Learn to identify them, know where their habitats are located, and avoid them.

■ Creatures living in or around the water, such as certain species of poisonous frogs, crocodiles and alligators, hippos, tigers and bears. Know how best to evade direct confrontation.

■ Camp followers and thieves of the animal variety such as racoons and monkeys who become a nuisance to others if you encourage them.

CROCODILES ARE ONE OF THE LURKING DANGERS THAT MAY THREATEN YOUR PEACE AND SAFETY ON A RIVER TRIP. ASCERTAIN THE LIKELIHOOD OF THEIR PRESENCE IN THE REGION BEFOREHAND, AND TAKE SENSIBLE PRECAUTIONS IN ORDER TO AVOID DIRECT CONFRONTATION.

Boat Control

'You can dance with the river, but you've got to know the steps.'
— Jerome Truran *(explorer of the Amazon and Colca rivers, Peru)*

at the heart of whitewater rafting is the set of skills seasoned river-runners call 'boating', meaning proper boat control in turbulent water. Moving water is powerful and will sweep you along out of control unless you master the skills of manoeuvring in waves, currents and rocky channels. Everything starts with reading the river (see pp 24 — 38). But planning your line through a rapid is not the same as actually making that line.

Remember that rivers are constantly in process. A rapid that from the bank looks like a fixed course may turn out to be much wilder and less manageable when you are in the middle of it. Fortunately, since water behaves fairly predictably, it's possible to learn boat control even in the biggest water.

As you start working on your skills, it helps to remember some general principles. River-running is a 'head game'. It's all about observing the river, knowing your limits, having confidence in your true abilities, planning your moves and communicating with others.

There is no training substitute for 'river time'. The river is certainly a tough teacher, if you are determined to learn the hard way. Yet you can pick up important lessons from a mentor, whose advice is valuable in direct proportion to the experience he or she has gained on the river.

A floating log will get down almost any kind of river eventually, but if you want to accomplish your run with a bit more elegance than a log, work on technique. The most basic strokes require constant practice to carry out manoeuvres sharply on demand.

opposite page NEW RAFT DESIGNS HAVE PRODUCED A WIDE VARIETY OF INFLATABLE BOATS TO SUIT BOTH AMATEUR AND EXPERIENCED RAFTERS, SUCH AS THESE BEING USED ON A TRIP ON THE COLORADO RIVER, USA.

If paddling with a crew, use a calm stretch for team building. Although the river is very forgiving, there are times it loses patience and that is when you need every ounce of your nerve and ability. You may be trounced all the same. Pick yourself out of the foam and carry on with the thought that the river is really quite neutral and you are tackling it by personal choice.

Finally — and this is not advice you hear very often — the microcurrents near your boat are as important as the macro currents forming the body of the rapid. Boat control depends very much on refining your reading of the river to the point where just the right move makes all the difference to your line. A deft oar stroke or planting your paddle in an eddy beside the boat can ensure a faultless run, although the water all around may seem chaotic.

Much river time may pass before you feel that you have a respectable level of boat control in wild water. The first step is to choose the right boat, and know what you are getting into with different types of raft.

Rafts today

A raft is essentially a floating platform. Originally a construction lashed together from logs, rafts were either prodded along by a long pole or dragged across the river by ropes, ferrying people and goods from bank to bank. Today's modern inflatables are nothing like this, but their link with the past is seen in their astonishing load capacity.

During the 1950s, the classic 'rubber raft' came onto the market as army surplus after World War II and was used by thousands of North Americans to explore the continent's whitewater rivers. Although manufactured for troop landings and commando raids, these boats proved ideal for river-running. Recently, the conventional idea of a rounded oblong boat with inflated

chambers has been challenged with the introduction of strange new raft designs. While some may seem freakish, adventurers are using them to push the margins of whitewater experience well beyond what was considered possible only a generation ago. A combination of improved materials and better understanding of river physics has produced an upsurge in design and a wide variety of choices.

Your choice of raft

There are many factors to consider when choosing a raft. Will you carry it on your car? What kinds of rivers do you plan to run? How much can you afford? Do you want it for family outings on mild rivers or for trips with some hardy friends to challenge raging waters? The answers will determine your most sensible choice, based on portability, performance, load capacity, cost and maintenance. A list of requirements is essential, especially when purchasing over the Internet — an increasingly popular buying option. Get advice from actual users and pepper the manufacturer with ques-

tions. Your main concerns are how rugged the material is (for scraping over rocks and buckling when tons of water dump on you); how easily it can be repaired using glues or welding techniques; and whether it resists the effects of ultraviolet radiation.

Ideally, one should buy a new raft but sometimes you may hear about a second-hand bargain through the grapevine. Look, listen and smell for signs of strained or ruptured seams; chambers that hiss or have been patched many times; mouldy odours from inside the chambers; or deterioration due to wear or sunlight. A properly inflated chamber should resound with a low 'boink' sound when slapped, and should not deflate overnight.

Raft construction materials

Inflatables are primarily made of fabrics covered with an abrasion-resistant, waterproof coating. In good materials, the underlying fabric is usually nylon or polyester that has been knitted or woven. 'Denier', a measurement of the threads in grams per 9000m of length, is used to rate fabric. In the past, higher 'denier' or fabric weight meant higher strength, but nowadays, one finds some very tough lighter materials with lower denier.

The coating on the fabric consists of synthetic rubber compounds (e.g. Hypalon, and less frequently, Neoprene); or newer plastomers such as polyvinyl chloride (PVC) and Urethane. An advantage of these new coatings is that they can be welded using heat and microwaves, while the other compounds must be glued. Urethane and Hypalon have generally been found to be the most resistant to the deteriorating effects of the sun's harsh ultraviolet rays.

APART FROM THE INFLATABLES SEEN HERE, SMALLER KAYAKS ARE ALSO POPULAR AMONG THE THOUSANDS OF WHITEWATER ENTHUSIASTS WHO RUN THE RAPIDS OF THE GRAND CANYON IN ARIZONA, USA.

RAFTS ON RIVERS HAVE THREE main functions: to carry passengers and loads, to run rapids and to float on flatwater stretches. They must combine buoyancy, lightness and carrying capacity with the ability to track in the water, turn, rise over waves and continue floating if capsized.

Some important features are:

■ **KICK:** The degree to which the ends are upturned. The greater the kick, the quicker the raft pivots, but the more likely it is to spin off a wave and possibly flip.

■ **WIDTH:** The wider the raft, the more stable it should be, but a narrower craft will negotiate narrower channels and turn more rapidly.

■ **CHAMBERS:** The tubes are divided into chambers. An oblong raft generally has four chambers. While larger tubes have better buoyancy, they can get cumbersome if they exceed 65cm (25in). That's because the boat is generally bigger and requires longer chambers.

■ **THWARTS:** These cross tubes lend rigidity to the inflatable boat and give it more buoyancy.

■ **VALVES:** An important element of the raft, good valves are recessed to avoid injury to crew. They should allow air to pass rapidly and efficiently when inflating or deflating the tubes. Valves should not have to be unscrewed, but should work by being pressed in and released thereafter.

■ **D-RINGS:** These hold the handlines and take a lot of strain when the boat is wrapped on a rock and has to be pulled off. D-Ring assemblies comprise the ring held by a durable flap, and cemented into a tough foundation patch.

■ **SELF-BAILING FLOOR:** Floors are both inflated and laced in, or attached with drainage holes along the edge. Some believe that rafts should not be self-bailing because the added weight of the water in the raft gives it solidity when hitting large waves; but self-bailers are more manoeuvrable.

■ **OAR FRAMES:** Made of wood or alloy, the frame provides the mount for oarlocks or pins to which the oars are attached. Frames also provide a seat for the oarsman and allow a webbing net or rigid floor to be suspended into the raft body for packing gear. There are two oarlock systems: U-shaped oarlocks, which are flexible and allow the oar to spring out under stress; and pins or 'thole pins' that rotate, allowing the oar to be clipped onto the mount and stay fixed in place in rough water. Thole pins keep your oar at the correct angle.

■ **OARS AND PADDLES:** Oar length is based on the width of the raft. Ideally, roughly a third of the oar should be between one's hand and the oarlock. Paddles should be long enough to put the paddle grip at nose level when you are sitting on the tube, with the whole paddle blade immersed in the water.

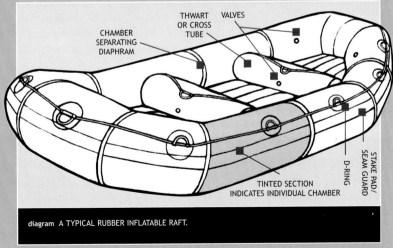

CHAMBER SEPARATING DIAPHRAM

THWART OR CROSS TUBE

VALVES

STAKE PAD/ SEAM GUARD

D-RING

TINTED SECTION INDICATES INDIVIDUAL CHAMBER

diagram A TYPICAL RUBBER INFLATABLE RAFT.

Types of Rafts

■ RIG

The biggest multipassenger rafts — generally called 'rigs' — consist of pontoons held together with transom frames. There are many types of rigs, and they are virtually impossible to flip. Not surprisingly, rigs are popular with tourists in the big rapids of the Grand Canyon and Fraser River. Rigs usually have a motor suspended at the back of the cutaway middle pontoons. The motor can be lifted up in shallow water to allow the rig to drift or be pulled along using oars. Many rigs have side tubes for added stability, allowing them to carry more passengers.

■ OARBOAT

There are two types of oarboats — inflatable oar rafts, and hard-hulled drift boats (dories). The front and back sections carry passengers. The oarsman who runs the boat through the rapids is usually an expert, or soon learns to be. A peculiarity of oarboats on rivers is that the oarsmen will often turn their boats so that they are looking forwards as they go downstream. The stroke used to row forward is called the 'Portegee', or Galloway, position.

MOTOR POWERED RIGS ARE ESPECIALLY POPULAR WITH LARGE RAFTING GROUPS ON COMMERCIALLY-RUN RIVERS.

PONTOON RAFTS DWARF A 5M (18 FT) WOODEN DORY BOAT ON THE COLORADO RIVER, IN ARIZONA, USA.

■ OAR RAFT

The oars in an oar raft are normally pivoted on rowlocks or a thole pin. This is mounted on a metal or wooden frame cinched to the top of the raft tubes. The frame is a major feature of the oar raft. It creates load space inside the raft, making these boats well suited for carrying boxes of food, bags, and camping equipment on longer trips.

■ DORY

In a dory, the oarsman sits amidships with the passengers on other benches forward and aft. The theoretically water-proof chambers below decks are used for storage. Dories are the descendants of the first wooden boats to run the Grand Canyon in the late 1860s. In those days, however, the oarsman sat with his back to the rapids while rowing the boat.

■ PADDLE RAFT

In this raft everyone manoeuvres the boat downriver by paddling together as a member of the crew under a skipper. Paddle rafts are versatile; they can be used for different types of trips as well as for both big water and shallow rivers. The short reach of paddles makes these boats suitable for smaller, tighter rivers. However, they flip more easily than oarboats

LIGHTWEIGHT INFLATABLE CANOES TO SEAT ONE OR TWO PADDLERS ARE POPULAR THROUGHOUT THE WORLD. THESE HARDY 'CROCODILES' ARE USED WITH DOUBLE-BLADED PADDLES AND WERE DEVELOPED FOR ROCKY, NARROW RIVERS WITH BIG RAPIDS.

and require skilled captaincy in tricky channels. Paddle rafts generally do not have frames but on expeditions it is more convenient to have a frame that holds dry boxes and other gear.

■ CATARAFT

The cataraft emerged in the late 1980s as the boat of choice for thrill-seekers. It consists of two inflated snout pontoons with turned-up ends held together by a metal frame. A single oarsman can handle a small cataraft and the boat can be paddled, oared or both. Sometimes two paddlers take the front with an oarsman using a sweep oar as a rudder at the back or two oars in the normal

way to increase power. Catarafts can carry a smallish load but are generally used for sport rather than transport.

■ INFLATABLE CANOE

Built with the same materials as bigger rafts, but more suited to getting down smaller rivers, inflatable canoes of various kinds have appeared in several regions including Australia and the Americas. These inflatable boats are built for long hauls carrying loads for longer trips.

Born on Southern Africa's shallow, rocky rivers, the two-person inflatable canoe or 'Crocodile' is very hardy, even withstanding attacks by hippos and crocodiles.

New trends in design

■ INFLATABLE KAYAK

These single-seater, banana-shaped inflatables confirm the modern trend in riverboat design towards smaller, zippier craft. The inflatable kayak is extremely manoeuvrable and, unlike the hard-hulled kayak variety, tends to be very stable. Using double-bladed paddles for propulsion, the paddler sits on the inflated floor held by a backrest and knee straps. The boat has been used to run steep mountain creeks. Ordinary kayakers have grudgingly conceded that it is a boat for all rivers. The latest decked inflatable kayaks are almost as rigid as hardshells, and their self-bailing floors mean they never have to be emptied.

DESPITE ITS OUTLANDISH APPEARANCE, THIS BUBLIK BEING USED BY WHITEWATER ENTHUSIASTS ON THE OYGAING RIVER IN UZBEKISTAN IN RUSSIA, IS SAFE EVEN IN WILD WATER.

■ PADDLECAT

On this racy craft the crew sit astride the pontoons and take the river full in the face. They paddle in tandem with two, four or even six people. Russian rafters first developed home-made paddlecats to run wild, unexplored rivers, and after the USA — Russian Chuya Rally in the late 1980s, the technology spread to America. The boat is highly manoeuvrable and can handle big rapids though it gives a wet ride.

Innovative designs

Many exciting modern concepts are hitting the river, some to float new business enterprises while others may sink and be forgotten. These designs offer a wide variety to suit both beginners and extreme rafters.

■ SOLO-CAT

Based on the catamaran principle, but with the smaller shape and size of a kayak, solo-cats are nimble warriors in the water. They combine a rigid frame with stiff, inflated tubes, and as the boat has no deck or bottom it is naturally self-bailing. Like other kayaks, they can get down very shallow rivers. Solo-cats are reasonably stable and are suitable for beginners.

■ HYDRO-BRONC

Comprising a sphere of seven inflated tubes, the hydro-bronc requires its occupant to move like a hamster inside a treadmill. Known generically as wheelrafts, these and similar innovative whitewater inflatables literally roll downriver and are able to bounce over rocks and Grade 6 rapids without mishap. In this boat you'll get plenty of aerobic exercise working your legs and holding onto the internal handles, so they demand a high level of fitness.

BUBLIK

The Russian bublik is another, rather freakish, type of wheelraft. It seems able to stay safe and upright even in big holes. First made by Soviet river-runners from surplus materials, the bublik — the Russian word for bread ring — consists of two large inner tubes joined by a platform or poles.

HYDROSPEED

For full body immersion, nothing beats the hydrospeed, developed by French paddlers and resembling a sturdy plastic bobsled that floats. The user dons scuba diving fins, a reinforced neoprene wetsuit, a helmet and a personal flotation device (PFD) to plunge down spine-tingling stretches of river. Hydrospeeds have been used to run the Amazon (South America) and explore mountain creeks in the Alps and Andes.

BODYBOARDS and SURFBOARDS

An old concept imported from the beach to the river, boards of various kinds are being used to surf waves on the Zambezi (Southern Africa), the Snake River (Idaho) and elsewhere. Where hydrospeeders swim downriver, boarders stay just where they are: unless they get blasted off the wave and carried away.

Others on the water

Apart from inflatable rafts — otherwise known as 'floaters' — many kinds of riverboat ply the waters of the world, carrying fishermen, ferrymen, engineers, researchers and other recreational enthusiasts. Learn to respect these river users and get along with them. They are allies in the ongoing struggle to save endangered rivers around the world.

Although rafters pour scorn on powerboats, they have their uses. Operators increasingly make use of powerboats to rescue swimmers at the ends of rapids.

Powered rafts or rubber ducks can go where floaters cannot — for example, the foot of the Albert Falls on the White Nile (Uganda), where the powered rubber duck is able to cruise on very wild water.

Hovercraft have the amazing ability to go *up* rapids, floating on a cushion of air and driven by a fan. In the 1970s, hovercraft went up rivers in the Himalayas. They have also been used on the Blue Nile in Ethiopia. The most common fellow travellers on whitewater trips are kayaks and canoes. Kayaks often perform as scouts and rescue boats.

Floater rafts are widely acknowledged to have right of way on rivers. Other boats must get out of the way or be run over.

Pumps

The most critical accessory on the river is your raft pump — lose or damage it and you will know the meaning of lung-power. It is possible to blow up smaller rafts with your breath but this is the last extremity for those who should be better prepared for a whitewater trip.

TYPES OF PUMPS

- Compressors, running off electrical power or combustion engines, are used at base or at the put-in, but are rarely taken downriver.
- Lightweight electrical pumps may be carried downriver to run off batteries or small generators.
- Handpumps and footpumps are convenient for use on longer rafting trips.

TAKING CARE OF YOUR PUMP

- Always carry several pumps with spare hoses. Take precautions to keep them clean and free of water.
- Do not use them for water games. This is because muddy or dirty water will convey grit into the compression chamber and damage the delicate rings that seal the plunger mechanism of the pump.
- When using a handpump, use long, smooth strokes, taking care not to jerk the device.
- The same technique applies to foot pumps, which will wear at the seams if roughly handled.
- Never blow up a raft with a hose attached to the exhaust pipe of a motor vehicle. It will damage the raft fabric and the hot air is likely to stretch the seams.

Raft design and accessories

Going with the flow

Seemingly minor differences between the profiles of raft hulls can change the handling of the boat significantly.

Let's examine some of them (See diagram below). When the floor joining the two chambers is raised, creating a concave profile under the raft (A), the chambers act like rudders. This gives the boat what is called directional stability: it stays on course. The downside is that it does not turn as easily as the raft with a flush bottom (B). Flush-bottomed rafts tend to waddle or yaw when rowing power is applied on one side or the other of the boat.

The pontoon craft (C), which has no floor at all, keeps its direction very well although it has little load capacity. Because it is light and floats high on the water, this sporting boat tends to turn easily. The slightly convex floor of the inflatable kayak (D) keeps it on track, but because the raft is short and very light, it turns at almost every stroke.

Packing loads

It's always good to see a well-packed raft, with all the items from dry boxes to clothing bags stowed away under tight tie-downs. Ensure that nothing

IF THE BOAT SHOULD CAPSIZE OR ENCOUNTER TURBULENT WATER, ITEMS ARE LIKELY TO BE LOST UNLESS THEY ARE SECURELY TIED DOWN AND STOWED AWAY IN THE RAFT.

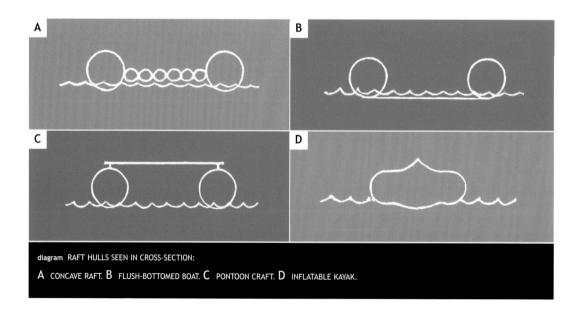

diagram RAFT HULLS SEEN IN CROSS-SECTION:

A CONCAVE RAFT. B FLUSH-BOTTOMED BOAT. C PONTOON CRAFT. D INFLATABLE KAYAK.

comes loose and no one can get snagged in trailing lines or nets if the raft capsizes.

Modern rowing frames have fittings for dry boxes, ammunition cans, medical boxes, day boxes and the other paraphernalia that is carried downriver. Paddle boats and inflatable canoes do not have frames, but use tie-downs attached to D-rings to secure the load. Expedition paddle rafts make use of frames in which a net may hang.

Heavier items should be packed in the middle of the boat, and softer ones placed on top. This prevents paddlers from being struck by hard edges if the raft bends.

Raft repair

Travel with a repair kit and know how to use it. Most raft manufacturers will provide a starter repair kit and supply detailed instructions on how to patch punctured chambers. Repairing holes and rips on the river is always tricky because it's difficult to find a clean, dry, well-lit area. You may have to replace the patches back at base. A parted seam is a major problem. As a 'quick-fix' measure, you can 'suture' it with needle and nylon thread, and place a temporary patch over it.

Wash the fabric thoroughly with thinners and roughen it, bevelling the edges of the patch to make it flush with the raft chamber. After marking the border with a felt-tip pen, apply the adhesive to both surfaces and allow it to dry.

Carefully roll the patch on using a spoon or hard roller. Conventional glues usually take several hours to dry (longer in cold climates) and may take as long as 72 hours to cure. Fortunately, the latest adhesives dry quickly, thus enabling you to pump the raft within an hour or two.

Humidity and dust are particular problems. Hot sun can do serious damage to fully inflated rafts, so keep them cool and wet and deflate during lunch hour stops if necessary.

Using oars and paddles

Your arms, shoulders, stomach, back and legs, and even the balls of your feet, provide the raft's 'motor power'. The body should act like a giant spring, transferring the impulse of the muscles to the face of the oar or paddle. All too often, though, people row with their arms only. Not only is this inefficient, it is also exhausting.

When the blade is planted in the water it should stay there while your body rotates, thrusting the boat onward. If only your arms move, the rowing or paddling motion will not be carried through the spine into the boat. The blade will merely sweep past the boat, instead of the boat going past the blade. By putting your shoulders and back into the stroke, you will have more power and greater control.

The safety talk and demo

Launching in

Because rafting is participatory and everyone in the group is at risk, it is essential to give a safety talk at the start of every rafting trip. This may seem unnecessary if people have heard it all before, but it is not. Rivers differ, trip leaders want to make particular points, and reminders are often useful.

The safety talk has been called the most important 20 minutes on the river. Usually given when people have finished packing and have chosen their boats and companions, it must have the attention of the whole group. The trip leader, a senior guide, or an experienced paddler (on private trips) should give it.

If you have not heard a safety talk before, it is a basic list of do's and don'ts. If you have to give the talk yourself, the format would be to say it, show it, involve the group and allow time for questions. People may be nervous and should be encouraged with positive statements about the river, but no one should be left in any doubt about the important basics of safety, ethics and minimum impact.

The safety talk for a day tour can be very brief but longer trips or higher-grade rivers need a more elaborate introduction. Use this outline for your talk:

SAY IT!

After introducing the leader and guides, describe the river route. Reminder: the trip is undertaken at own risk. Be careful and responsible.

■ Establish if anyone is a nonswimmer, has a physical disability or medical condition, is very nervous, or is on any treatment. Discuss privately if necessary.

■ Establish if anyone is a doctor, nurse or paramedic. Point out the medical box.

■ Remind people to wear safety gear.

Rescues

■ Rescues are likely and an incident commander is appointed for major rescues. Show the signals for 'Are you okay?' and 'Emergency help needed' (see p 52).

■ People should not get involved unless asked.

SHOW IT!

■ If possible, stand above a rapid and discuss the current, tongue, eddies, eddy fences, standing waves, holes, cushions, strainers, boulder sieves and other features. Explain 'upstream', 'downstream', 'river left' and 'river right'.

■ Demonstrate rope throwing and show how a swimmer should hold a rope, while kicking and lying on his/her back.

■ Demonstrate paddle signals and ask everyone to repeat them using their own paddles.

DO IT!

■ Allocate crews and skippers to boats, show crew how to sit holding their paddles correctly (Diagram 1), and explain how loads are stowed and secured.

Safety Warnings

■ Never get ahead of the lead guide or fall behind the sweep. You may always call a halt and ask to scout a rapid or walk around.

■ Never attempt to shoot a rapid alone and unless support is on hand.

■ Never paddle or hike away from the party without informing the trip leader or deputy beforehand, and do not go alone.

■ Never tie yourself to a raft or attach a line to any part of your body while rafting, swimming or wading.

■ Never jump from rock to rock or jump onto piles of driftwood when scouting from the bank. Step carefully.

■ Never jump or dive in the river unless you have checked that it is deep enough.

■ Do not use paddles in waterfights or pull anyone into the water. Never board or capsize other boats.

■ Never drink unpurified river water, even from creeks and springs that seem clear.

■ Never drag rafts over the ground; carry them. Wash off your sandals or bootees before stepping in the raft — this may bring grit and thorns into the boat.

■ Show how to wedge feet lightly in foot cups or under thwarts, and point out the risks of hooking legs and feet in lines or under loads (Diagram 2).

■ Get in the boats, first on the bank and then on the water, and work through rafting commands: Forward! Back! Stop! Hold! Draw!

■ Teach turning (see p 54) and high siding (see p 56), first on the bank, then on the water.

■ Teach forward and reverse ferry gliding across the current (see p 57).

Personal kit and boats

■ Check everyone's PFDs and helmets for fit and comfort. Wear PFDs at all times, and don helmets (if issued) in rapids.

■ Make sure everyone is allocated to a boat, has paddles, has packed their bags and has not left any of their belongings behind.

■ If wearing spectacles, tie them on.

■ Check people have sun blockout and have a windcheater handy for cold weather.

Minimum impact

■ Use the toilet facilities provided and burn or bag the paper. Do not urinate in the river. Do not build bonfires or use driftwood. Carry cigarette butts away with you when you leave.

Warnings if swimming

■ Do not stand up or wade in moving water above the knees.

■ Do not swim towards trees. If you are washed into branches or logs in the river, reach up and pull your body out of the water into the tree.

■ If caught in a hole (hydraulic), make an effort to swim for the side or eye. Do not remove your lifejacket unless all else fails, because rope rescue may be on hand.

■ When swimming downriver, breathe in at the troughs between waves and not at the peaks.

■ Whenever swimming, try to rescue yourself by reaching a calm eddy or rock ledge.

■ Always wash away from the river, using biodegradable soaps.

■ Please respect landowners' rights and privacy.

Harmful substances

■ Do not drink alcohol or take drugs during the day on the river. These substances often make people uncoordinated, reckless or sleepy.

■ Anyone on medication should report it to the trip leader or deputy and discuss the implications.

diagram 1 SIT COMFORTABLY WITH THE LEGS INBOARD, HOLDING THE PADDLE FIRMLY BY ITS T-GRIP AND SHAFT. USE YOUR SHOULDERS AND BODY TO TRANSFER FORCE TO YOUR ARMS AND HANDS.

diagram 2 TUCK ONE OR BOTH FEET UNDER THE THWART BUT DO NOT SLIDE THEM IN TOO FAR AND BE CAREFUL NOT TO GET STUCK. MANY RAFTS HAVE FOOT-CUPS.

River Signals

VISUAL SIGNALS ARE USED ON THE river because people at a distance can respond to them. Calling instructions seldom work as words are often lost or muffled in the noise of rapids.

Signals are usually given by the scout from downriver to those wanting to proceed. One person in each boat or those on the bank must reply to every signal.

Signals may be used as questions, for example, asking with a raised paddle, 'Can we come?' The reply might be a raised paddle ('Yes'), a horizontal paddle ('No'), or a directional paddle pointing one way or another ('Go that way'). Hand signals are the same as for paddles. The diamond hand signal (G), 'OK to come down the middle and scout as you go', means choose your own way downriver. Stand up in the raft if necessary to get a better look.

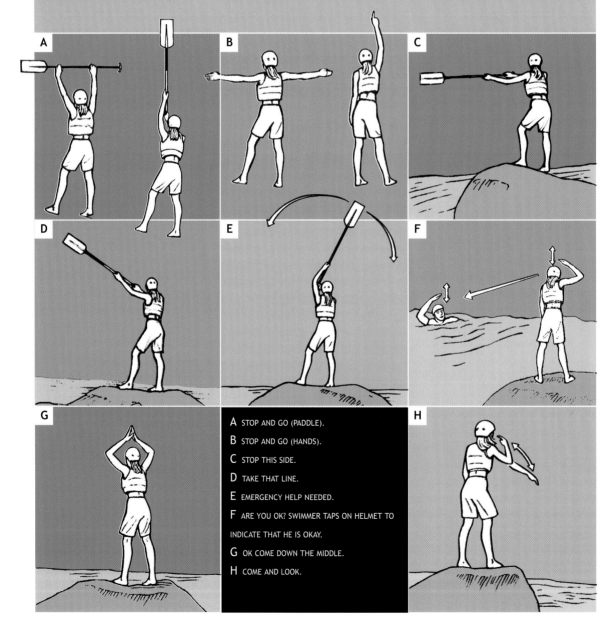

A STOP AND GO (PADDLE).

B STOP AND GO (HANDS).

C STOP THIS SIDE.

D TAKE THAT LINE.

E EMERGENCY HELP NEEDED.

F ARE YOU OK? SWIMMER TAPS ON HELMET TO INDICATE THAT HE IS OKAY.

G OK COME DOWN THE MIDDLE.

H COME AND LOOK.

Safety

TRIP ROLES

For the sake of overall safety and more efficient inter-action on the river, there are well-known roles and routines that should be adhered to by anyone undertaking a whitewater trip. When each member of the group knows the importance of the roles played by key crew, risks can be minimized and accidents are less likely.

■ **THE GROUP:** No one should get ahead of the lead guide (scout) or behind the back marker (sweep).
A medical kit should be on each raft, and a full medical/emergency kit should also go with the first raft down the rapid.

■ **SCOUT:** The scout is a safety kayaker or skipper of the lead raft who precedes the party approaching a rapid. No matter how familiar the river is, the scout takes nothing for granted and looks out for marker rocks, fluctuations in water level, unexpected hazards (like logjams), and sudden changes in the river after floods. If the rapid looks serious, the scout signals people to stop, walk down and inspect it.

■ **SWEEP:** The person at the back of the group should be an experienced river hand. The sweep's main responsibility is to watch everyone and send them down rapids in orderly fashion.

■ **DECISION TIME:** With the rapid scouted, it is time to decide who goes and who does not. It is really up to each individual, but in marginal cases the leader, deputy or safety officer should provide necessary guidance to the rest of the group.

■ **RESCUE SET-UP:** Rescue boats and possibly people with rescue throwlines are positioned in or below the rapid to look after swimmers. Good signalling and speed of reaction are vital.

■ **PICK-UP MISSION:** If a rapid flips any boats, then swimmers, kit, paddles and boats could be all over the place. Before the sweep leaves the scene, rescuers have to spot and carefully collect missing items, or expensive paraphernalia will be lost.

■ **EMERGENCIES:** In the unusual event of a serious accident, certain casualty handling routines come into play. An incident commander takes over and various scenarios of rescue or recovery may be played out. These are dealt with on pp 62 – 77.

Catching a throwrope

The thrower shouts 'Rope!' to attract attention and tries to land the rope slightly downriver of the swimmer, who will catch up with it because it floats a little slower.
The swimmer grabs the throwrope and immediately rolls over onto his or her back, in order to plane on the surface of the water.

Don't hold the throwrope while lying on your chest — when the rope is pulled you will be dragged headlong into the turbulent current of the water.

Remember never to wrap the rope around your wrist or body. You must be able to let go. This is extremely dangerous because the rope can snag on rocks or trees and a person who is entangled becomes a 'deadman anchor' trailing in the current.

Don't panic if your limbs or clothing get snagged in the rope — just unhitch them.

THE RESCUER HURLING A THROWROPE TO A SWIMMER IN DISTRESS IS AT SOME RISK ON A SLIPPERY HIGHPOINT, BUT THERE MAY BE NO ALTERNATIVE POSITION.

Swimming down a rapid

After a capsize there may be several swimmers in the water. You'll need to look after yourself as immediate rescue is somewhat unlikely.

■ If and when you fall in, keep your feet near the surface to avoid snagging them in rocks.

■ Float downriver feet first with the knees slightly bent and the arms wide — as if you were holding a cocktail glass in each hand. The so-called 'cocktail' position gives you stability and allows you to stroke backwards as you make for safety.

■ Use your feet, thighs and bottom to deflect any rocks. As soon as you can see an opportunity to reach an eddy or the bank, roll over and swim hard.

■ Do not stand up in moving water deeper than your knees: rather pull yourself along on your belly, keeping the body and legs horizontal.

Hauling a swimmer on board

People who fall overboard should avoid swimming the rapid if possible. Quick retrieval of swimmers can prevent injuries in the water.

Everyone should learn how to haul a swimmer onboard because the skipper may be steering and unable to come to the swimmer's assistance. Shout at a swimmer to approach the raft, offering the paddle as an aid. Grab the shoulder straps of the PFD and lean backwards or fall into the raft pulling the swimmer after you. Hold the shoulder straps of the PFD, taking care NOT to pull the person by the arms as this can cause strains or dislocation.

Boating strokes

Boaters — at least those who do the work — get down-river by their own efforts with a bit of help from the river. Muscle power applied to paddles or oars is what gets you where you want to go. All riverboats need to execute basically the same manoeuvres, but as the strokes differ we shall look at oarboats, paddle rafts and inflatable kayaks separately. Navigation in running water usually involves a combination of these moves, adapted to the shape of your raft.

The key boating manoeuvres are (see diagram below):

■ **Track:** Staying on track means travelling forwards or backwards in a given direction (A). If a boat fails to stay on track it is said to wander or 'yaw'.

■ **Turn:** A boat that is tracking can follow an arc and so turn while still making headway (B).

■ **Pivot:** A boat pivots when it remains in one spot but rotates on its axis (C).

■ **Ferry:** A boat is ferrying when it forges against the current at an angle, thus letting the current push it sideways across the river (D). This concept is explained further on p 57.

■ **Crest:** Inflatables tend to crest the waves rather than diving right through them (E). Rafts, although buoyant, can be tipped over by big waves.

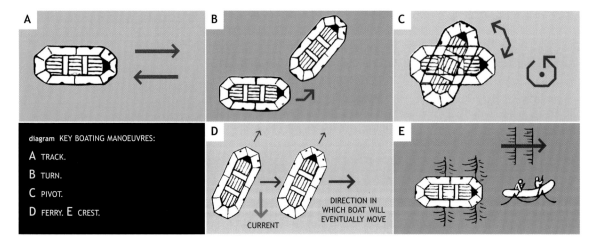

diagram KEY BOATING MANOEUVRES:
A TRACK.
B TURN.
C PIVOT.
D FERRY. E CREST.

CURRENT

DIRECTION IN WHICH BOAT WILL EVENTUALLY MOVE

BEFORE YOU KNOW IT, THE RAFT has flipped and you are in the water. This can happen anytime in rapids — it does not take a big wave or rock to capsize the boat, just incorrect weight displacement of the crew.

On cold rivers, the idea of doing a capsize drill and getting wet is never popular. But if the river throws rapids at you from the start, a drill (or at least a detailed explanation and practice on the bank) is necessary.

On warm days people are happy to swim after the safety talk. Select a pool with moving water and go through the capsize drill routine shown, starting with a deliberate flip (A). With everyone in the water, the skipper must count heads or call out names to ascertain that everyone is on the water surface and that there are no problems (B).

In wild water, don't spend time reflipping a heavy raft: pull people onto the upturned bottom. The crew can paddle like this to safety (C).

If you come up beneath a capsized raft, air may be trapped between the chambers and the water surface. It is possible to breathe. Feel your way along, keeping your legs as near the surface as possible.

Swim out beside the raft (D), getting away from the downstream end of it, as there is a danger of body pinning, or being squashed against rocks.

Where the raft cannot be easily or quickly reflipped, the crew may climb on top of it (E) to run through the rest of the rapid. As soon as possible, the skipper should reflip the raft (F). The flipline, worn around the waist, is clipped to the raft and the skipper falls backwards, pulling the boat over.

If you snag your feet in ropes and boatloads or become entangled, try not to panic. Reach for the snagged limb, shoe or clothing and carefully unhitch it.

In extreme cases the skipper or someone with a knife may have to cut away the entanglement underwater. This would be an emergency, prompted by noticing that someone is missing.

THE RIVER IS UP, THE DAY FULL of promise. It is time to put your paddling techniques and knowledge of river dynamics to the test. If the river is rapid-strewn, your mind and energies will be engaged in reading the water, analyzing what you see, manoeuvring to put your boat where you want it to be, and recovering from any miscalculations (which are easy to make).

High-siding

Any raft, from large oarboats to dinky inflatables, can capsize if it tilts too far over.

As a general principle, if you are about to hit a wave or rock, never lean away from it. Rather greet the wave and lean towards the rock: aggressively throw all your weight onto the side that is lifting — the 'high side'. Practise on the bank first.

A lunge man can be positioned near the bow of the raft to execute a single strong stroke, hefting the boat over the wave (A).

High-siding (see diagram below) may require the involvement of the whole crew. As you approach the wave the skipper shouts 'High side' and everyone piles on top of each other (B), with the skipper finally adding his own weight (C). Beware of paddles hitting people across the face; remember to stretch arms out with paddles forward and away. As the raft crests and drops down the wave, fall back or you may tumble off into the trough. The lunge man may have to get ready for another wave (D).

Surfing

Not only surfers dream of the perfect wave. The river's standing waves afford wonderful opportunities for raft surfing, known as playboating. There are times when these techniques, perfected for fun, are useful in running rapids — and may save you from the direst consequences of a mistake.

Boaters can take a pause in a rapid even when there are no eddies for protection, by surfing a small stopper. The raft will tend to yaw, spin and side-surf against the foam pile, so the crew must be quick to high side.

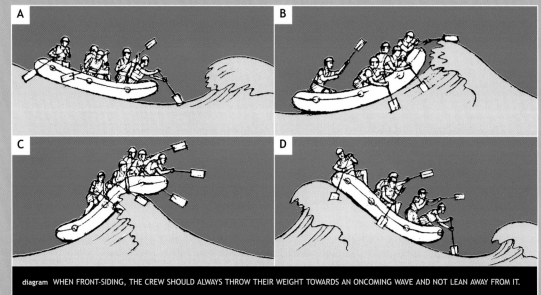

diagram WHEN FRONT-SIDING, THE CREW SHOULD ALWAYS THROW THEIR WEIGHT TOWARDS AN ONCOMING WAVE AND NOT LEAN AWAY FROM IT. THEY SHOULD REATHER LEAN TO AVOID BEING FLIPPED OVER BACKWARDS. HIGH-SIDING INVOLVES PILING SIDEWAYS INTO A LATERAL WAVE.

Use rudder strokes to keep the raft surfing forwards.

If faced with a monster hole, rafters should turn their boat upstream and surf across a standing wave just above the hole to reach open water. This takes split-second reactions.

Ferry gliding

Crossing the river to avoid hazards below is a standard and vital manoeuvre. It is surprising how a boat can cross, even in very strong currents, by using the power of the river to do so. The current pushing on the side of the boat will thrust it towards the bank, provided you hold your angle at between 20 and 35 degrees, pointing the boat where you want to go.

In ferrying you may either face upstream or downstream. It is quite easy to ferry

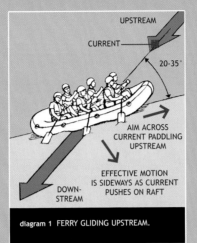

diagram 1 FERRY GLIDING UPSTREAM.

upstream (see Diagram 1), but downstream, or back-ferrying, takes more practice. Crews need to be very well drilled, and single oarsmen or paddlers must master ferrying to keep themselves out of trouble.

Eddy hopping

Beginners tend to see the river as a mass of water all moving in the same direction at the same speed. This is, however, far from being the case. A raft cruising down the main chute can break out of the main current into countercurrents, and even travel small distances back upriver. Descending a river using eddies as a kind of ladder is called eddy hopping (see Diagram 2).

When entering the rapid (A), the raft ferry glides facing upstream (B) in order to be rightly poised to enter the eddy (C). It crosses the eddy and lets the current turn the bow (D) in order to follow the current (E). With these moves it avoids bad holes across the river. As the boat enters the eddy (F), crew members need to be aware that strong counter-currents (eddy fences) can change the direction of the boat.

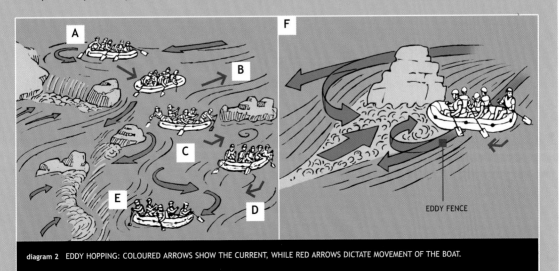

diagram 2 EDDY HOPPING: COLOURED ARROWS SHOW THE CURRENT, WHILE RED ARROWS DICTATE MOVEMENT OF THE BOAT.

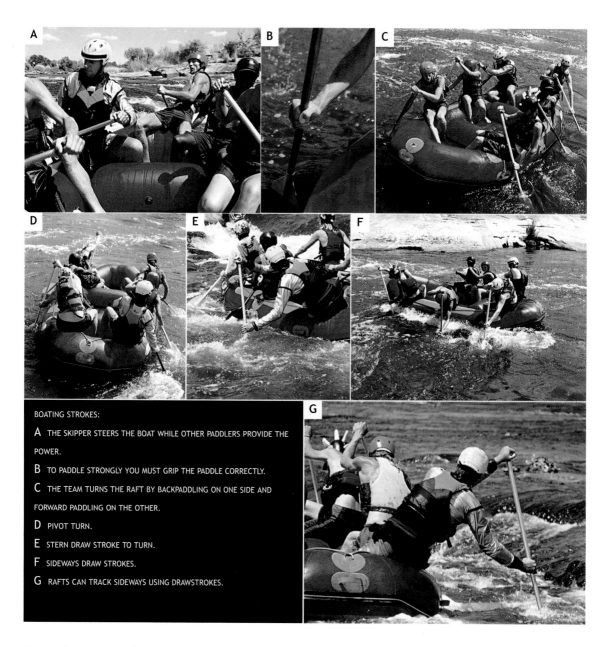

BOATING STROKES:

A THE SKIPPER STEERS THE BOAT WHILE OTHER PADDLERS PROVIDE THE POWER.

B TO PADDLE STRONGLY YOU MUST GRIP THE PADDLE CORRECTLY.

C THE TEAM TURNS THE RAFT BY BACKPADDLING ON ONE SIDE AND FORWARD PADDLING ON THE OTHER.

D PIVOT TURN.

E STERN DRAW STROKE TO TURN.

F SIDEWAYS DRAW STROKES.

G RAFTS CAN TRACK SIDEWAYS USING DRAWSTROKES.

Boating strokes

Oar Boats

In the early days of oarboating the rower sat with his back facing upriver. Boating was revolutionized when the rower turned round the face the rapid, and ran downriver pushing, rather than pulling, the oars. Now the oarsman could see what was coming and using 'Portegee' pushing strokes, could manoeuvre to miss rocks and holes.

Paddle rafts

With its ability to go everywhere and run almost everything, the ubiquitous paddle raft is a common sight on the world's rivers. These boats are very manoeuvrable and easy to handle if the crew is taught co-ordination and the skipper calls out clear, loud commands. The skipper sits at the stern (on the left or the right) and uses steering strokes while the crew provides power. Place at least one strong paddler near the bow to help with turning strokes. The crew needs to practise both front-siding (throwing their weight forward into an oncoming wave) and high-siding (piling sideways into a lateral wave). Do this in easy rapids so that it becomes instinctive in bigger water.

Smaller inflatables

Lighter, smaller single- and twin-seater inflatable craft are becoming the norm on many rivers. No longer regarded as toys, they have proved themselves in all kinds of water. Beginners can handle the racy inflatable kayaks, while inflatable canoes are suitable for expeditions because these boats are very stable and will crest over almost anything. They track, turn, pivot and ferry quite easily. In a smaller boat you are closer to the river and also learn faster than those in larger craft as you are forced to read the water in detail.

River physics

Boating involves a three-way relationship between the river, the raft and the crew. Without getting too technical, it helps to know a few principles of physics, and in particular, fluid dynamics.

SMALL INFLATABLES, LIKE THIS TWIN-SEATER, ARE POPULAR AS THEY ARE EXTREMELY MANOEUVRABLE AND VERSATILE.

Protect your shoulders

Shoulder dislocation, a common and agonizing injury in paddling, will completely incapacitate a person who experiences it for the first time. It can happen to rafters and especially inflatable kayakers when using the extended brace stroke (see Diagram 1). If the paddler's arm is outstretched backwards and a wave suddenly jerks the paddle blade upwards, the shoulder can easily pop forward out of its socket.

The low brace paddle position (see Diagram 2) protects the shoulder and is safer because the elbow is above the paddle and the arm ahead of the shoulder.

diagram 1 DANGEROUS SHOULDER MOVE.

diagram 2 SAFE SHOULDER MOVE.

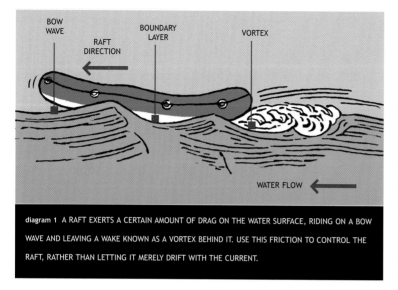

diagram 1 A RAFT EXERTS A CERTAIN AMOUNT OF DRAG ON THE WATER SURFACE, RIDING ON A BOW WAVE AND LEAVING A WAKE KNOWN AS A VORTEX BEHIND IT. USE THIS FRICTION TO CONTROL THE RAFT, RATHER THAN LETTING IT MERELY DRIFT WITH THE CURRENT.

The river

In Chapter 4 (see p 30), it was explained how the laminar flow of a placid river becomes turbulent when there is a sudden drop in the river, the channel constricts, and obstacles block the way.

■ In the zone of turbulence, the main current with its accompanying helicals encounters crosscurrents, undertow, eddies, whirlpools, boils and roils. These are the macro features of the rapid.

■ All these are frictioning against each other to create eddy 'fences' (see Diagram 2 on p 57).

■ Along these fences you will encounter swirls and wavelets, the micro features so important to boat control. By noticing where the fences or zones of shear are, you can interpret the interplay of currents and respond with decisive moves of your own.

The raft

Inflatables exhibit certain unique features and others that are typical of nautical hulls.

■ Typically (see Diagram 1), the pressure of the hull pushing against water creates a bow wave and a secondary wave. The area of direct friction is called the boundary layer, while behind the boat is a triangle of negative pressure called the vortex (this is, in fact, an eddy created by the boat itself). Friction and pressure give the raft traction on the water, which is very useful as it promotes manoeuvrability.

■ Unlike normal boats, rafts do not have rudders or keels (which would be knocked off by rocks), so steering is done by rowing. A hull gains the ability to manoeuvre when it moves faster or slower than the current. This is when it is necessary to use both forward and back paddling.

■ Rather uniquely, rafts are flexible. The hull often wallows in troughs and is squashed sideways by lateral waves. The raft also bends over waves. Its flexibility increases the drag of the water on the hull. It may be bounced backwards by waves and crew members may be flipped out when the hull flexes suddenly. So hold on, especially at the bow and stern.

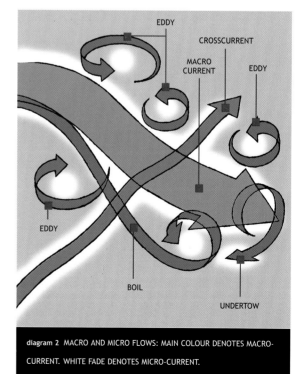

diagram 2 MACRO AND MICRO FLOWS: MAIN COLOUR DENOTES MACRO-CURRENT. WHITE FADE DENOTES MICRO-CURRENT.

THE LOGIC OF WHITEWATER manoeuvres appears to defy common sense. Yet there is such a thing as 'river logic' that implies using the power of the water to your own advantage.

If you want to miss a rock, point towards it. If you do hit a rock, lean onto it and hug it. This needs some explaining (see Diagram 3).

By pointing towards a rock (A) and allowing the boat's stern to swing out with the current (B), you allow the forces of the river to carry you around the obstacle (C). If and when you do broach against a rock, leaning onto it will keep the boat's upstream side out of the water. It will also prevent the boat from becoming submerged and wrapped against the rock.

Ferry gliding

Why do boaters so often ferry glide across the river, recross, spin their boats and hop into eddies? A little river physics explains why these manoeuvres may be needed to get you out of trouble.

The best whitewater navigators look 50 – 100m (roughly 55 – 110 yd) downriver and give themselves plenty of time to move into position. It is unwise to turn only at the last moment. If you don't consider the convergent currents that tend to push everything towards the middle of the river, your attempt to turn will fail.

A more effective strategy is to turn out of the main current at the top of the rapid, then ferry glide facing upstream.

This way, convergence works to the boater's advantage, pushing the raft sideways so that it is neatly positioned to pop into the eddy with just a firm pull on the oars. (In Diagram 3, a two-seater inflatable canoe is shown doing this). The boat will then turn out of the eddy and float downstream past the hole.

Bigger rafts may battle to turn and ferry glide facing upstream because they are heavy with more drag and resistance.

Ferry gliding puts a brake on the raft's progress, slowing it in relation to the current. This gives it traction or steerage way on the water.

All-round awareness

Good boaters analyze the river well because they have developed a panoramic vision of the raft and their surroundings.

Try to have four zones of awareness – the boat and crew, the micro-currents, the macro-currents, and the surrounding environment including the lie of the land and the weather.

Seeing things this way will help you to anticipate what is to come, while focusing on the micro-currents and the crew's state of mind.

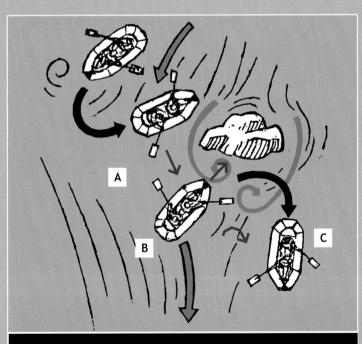

diagram 3 TO AVOID A HAZARD DOWNSTREAM, CROSS THE CURRENT. PIVOT THE BOAT TO FACE UPSTREAM AND USE EDDIES TO ENTER THE CURRENT AGAIN. BLUE ARROWS INDICATE THE CURRENT, RED, THE BOAT MANOEUVRE AND BLACK, THE EFFECTIVE DIRECTION OF THE BOAT.

Safety and Rescue

'Don't just stand there — panic!'(Sign at the entrance of a river guide training school)

a key principle in deciding to run a rapid is whether rescue is feasible. If it is not, or if rescue would involve a high degree of hazard to the rescuers, the rapid should be considered out of bounds for the average paddler. Even if rescue can be set up, this does not guarantee success when rescuers have to go into action.

Self-rescue (i.e. getting back in the boat, swimming for your life, wading out, or extricating yourself from a tricky situation) should always be attempted. Your best chance of survival is to look after yourself; but it would be extremely unwise to depend completely on self-rescue. At least two other tough and mentally prepared people should be on hand to render assistance in case a victim is unable to get out of trouble alone. In major rescues, teamwork under a capable incident commander (IC) is essential.

The purpose of rescue training is to prepare for the worst-case scenario. Although the principles of rescue are very simple, the practice can be very complex indeed. An easy-to-recall Rescue Action Plan (RAP) should form the framework for personal and team responses to typical situations (see p 69).

Rescue involves assisting a person to escape safely, though not necessarily uninjured, from a river hazard, while recovery applies to fetching equipment or, regrettably, a body, from the river.

Search and rescue means looking for people who have gone missing; *evacuation* occurs when members of a group leave an accident site and go to a safer area. Serious accidents and fatalities can and do occur. Statistically however, rafting is essentially a low-

> **opposite page** IT IS UNWISE TO RUN WILD RAPIDS WITHOUT HAVING A GOOD RESCUE ACTION PLAN IN CASE OF AN ACCIDENT.

Risk management

Rescue, like river-running itself, is a head game. Good rescuers are fast off the mark but they think before they react, knowing that ill-considered action causes further accidents. Sometimes rescuers take a calculated risk to retrieve equipment, because the risk of losing it outweighs the dangers of recovering it. For example, where a raft must be used to get out of a gorge, the motive is the survival of the group.

Keep in mind:

1. Risking a life to save a life could mean losing two lives.
2. Risking a life to save equipment may mean a senseless loss of life.
3. Risking a life to recover a body could result in a second fatality.

Risk management does not entail heroics. Take only calculated risks that do not expose the rescuer to the same hazard as the victim. Having a well worked out safety plan is the basic principle in all rescue scenarios.

fatality adventure sport which seldom involves truly life-threatening situations. The cushioning action of water against rocks and the fact that the river finds its own way past obstacles (carrying you with it) means that boaters and swimmers usually escape unharmed.

Swiftwater rescue requires intensive training and knowledge of ropework and emergency procedures. This guide focuses on techniques that can be applied by reasonably competent boaters, assuming that they have studied and practised the techniques under experienced leadership until they are proficient at them. If you are serious about leading trips, it is wise to consider enrolling for a course with an International Rafting Federation member association (see p 95).

Phases of River Rescue

PHASE	DURATION	PURPOSE	COMMENT
PHASE 1	0–30 seconds	Immediate escape from hazard	Self-rescue or fast team reaction to prevent consequences
PHASE 2	30 seconds– 2 minutes	Drowning prevention	The 'golden minutes' in which a drowning can be averted and the victim is given air
PHASE 3	2–8 minutes	Drowning intervention	The period in which a victim may be unconscious but still has a chance of resuscitation
PHASE 4	Immediate – 1 hour	Chase or proximate rescue	Time in which to stabilize the victim fully so as to effect rescue; or to follow and assist moving victims
PHASE 5	Over 1 hour	Continuing rescue effort	Rescues that take longer due to terrain, complex teamwork with ropes, or difficulty in extricating a victim
PHASE 6	Indefinite	Externally mounted search and rescue	The paddling group hands over incident command to rescue professionals but may remain to assist

Phase 1: In the first 30 seconds, self-rescue is most effective. One is likely to be conscious and able to reach safety, while others are not close enough to help.

Phase 2: The most crucial time is the so-called 'golden two minutes' it takes a person to become unconscious and then drown. In this period, reaching and helping victims to breathe is critical. Drowning may occur when water enters the lungs ('wet drowning') or when the larynx closes in a spasm and the person suffocates ('dry drowning'). In either case, closure of the airway first causes unconsciousness and finally death.

Phase 3: The time in which drowning is likely to occur can vary from less than two minutes to six minutes or much longer. Colder water slows down the metabolism, allowing oxygen to concentrate in the brain, and thus raises the chances of surviving without air even after prolonged immersion.

Phase 4: Victims swimming downriver definitely have time against them. Exposure to the elements may bring on life-threatening hypothermia (abnormally low body temperature).

Phase 5: The period in which a team continues its efforts to reach the victim. This phase, involving ropework, wading, swimming or boating, usually only ends once darkness sets in.

Phase 6: Where the team gives up or external help arrives. Once out of sight of rescuers, a victim must depend on self-rescue, but if he/she is injured or unconscious, this is not possible.

Think in terms of time

All rescuers are keenly concerned with time, because the longer it takes to reach someone in dire straits, the lower the chances of success.

Avoid, rescue, and review

The best river rescues are those that do not happen — simply because you avoided trouble in the first place. But if a rescue is necessary, learn from it.

■ **Pre-emptive safety** forestalls accidents when one carefully scouts the river and identifies risk sites that should be bypassed.

■ **Rescue assists** are fast interventions by helpers assisting someone with self-rescue (i.e. pulling them toward the raft with a paddle, or swimming with them into an eddy).

■ **Full rescue** is aimed at saving a victim from the hazards of the river. This may be done single-handedly or by a team.

■ **Discussing the rescue** is always advisable at the end of the rapid or at the end of the day. The team analyzes why pre-emptive safety failed, how the rescue progressed, and whether anything could be improved in future.

Rescue equipment

River rescue equipment — at least that carried by the leaders on whitewater trips — is by definition light-weight as heavy tackle slows one's reaction.

Essential items are:

■ **Rescue PFD:** This specialized personal flotation device has pockets for such items as surgical gloves and airway mouthpieces. Unlike the normal PFD, it comes with a fitted harness for abseiling (rapelling), a quick-release buckle for rescue swims, a belly pouch for a small medical kit and a throwbag on the back.

■ **Rescue kitbags:** These compact bags contain throwropes, carabiners, nuts and pulleys. Carry 100m (300ft) or more of coiled river ropes (polypropylene, which floats) for major rescues.

■ **Rescue throwbags:** These are the universal tools of rope rescue. A throwbag consists of a lightweight

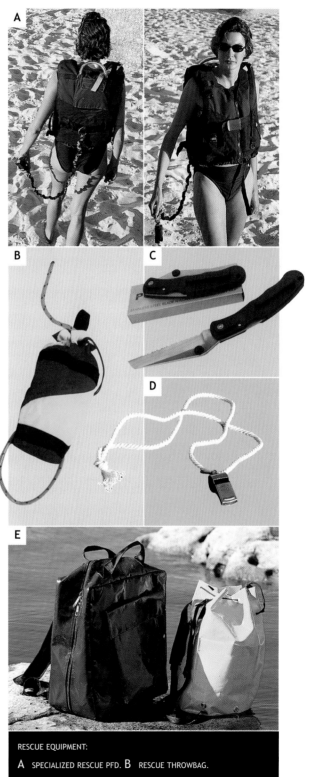

RESCUE EQUIPMENT:

A SPECIALIZED RESCUE PFD. B RESCUE THROWBAG.

C SHEATHKNIFE. D WHISTLE. E RESCUE KITBAGS.

pouch stuffed with rescue rope. The bag is held in the hand by a collar at the top, which is used to swing it and hurl it for great distances. The rope releases as the bag is thrown towards a swimmer, while the rescuer holds the end of the line.

■ **Frisbee throwbag**: A handy small throwbag, accessible with one pull on the backflap, is sold as a component of some lifejackets. These 'frisbees', thrown with a flick of the wrist, may only be 5 – 8m (15 – 25ft) long.

■ **Sheathknife on PFD**: Every rescuer must have a knife that either clicks into a sheath or has a blade that folds safely into the handle. You may need to use it to cut tangled ropes or even slash a pinned raft in a hurry. Secure the knife with a short elastic cord to prevent it being lost if it drops while being handled.

■ **Accessories**: Buy a good whistle and fit it to the PFD. It is handy to have a selection of prusik loops and webbing straps to use as connectors; anchors and belays for ropework; screwgate carabiners which cannot open if the rope twists; pulleys with running wheels for rigging haul lines; and climbing nuts for securing rope anchors in cracks in the rock. A roll of duct tape, sawtooth knife, mirror, and pliers or a multipurpose handyman tool are useful for general rescue situations and repair work.

■ **Personal medical kit**: While the group should have a complete medical box, a rescuer needs to carry a small first aid kit in a waterproof pouch or O-ring box along with a spare blanket for immediate care.

Rescue communications

Signals are imperative as soon as a rescue gets under way. Because it is often difficult to hear shouted instructions, people are more likely to see simple visual signals. These should not be misunderstood, and rescuers need to get into the habit of responding to a signal with the same 'Okay' signal, indicated by an arm pointed up (see Diagram A below). Show the desired action that you want , and people will under-stand that. If they do not, use the 'No way!' signal and repeat what you want until they understand.

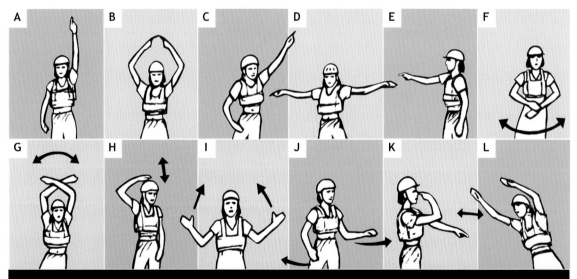

THE HAND SIGNALS HERE REPEAT SOME OF WHAT APPEARED EARLIER BUT WITH AN IMPORTANT DIFFERENCE: THEY MAKE SENTENCES FOR THOSE EXPERIENCED IN USING THEM.

A OKAY (TO COME/GO). (ARM POINTED UP.) B COME DOWN THE MIDDLE (DIAMOND SIGN.) C GO THAT WAY (POINTING DIRECTION TO TAKE.)

D STOP! (BOTH ARMS OUT.) E GO TO THAT BANK (ARM HORIZONTAL AND POINTING.) F DO NOT COME AT ALL! (ARMS WAVED ACROSS BODY.)

G HELP NEEDED HERE! (ARMS WAVING ABOVE HEAD.) H ARE YOU OKAY? (HAND PATS HELMET.) I UP! OUT OF THE BOAT! (THUMBS JERKING UPWARDS.)

J WALK! (SAWING MOTION OF HANDS.) K COME AND LOOK-SEE! (POINTING AT EYES.) L SWIM! (SHOW SWIMMING MOTION.)

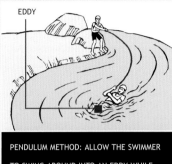

PENDULUM METHOD: ALLOW THE SWIMMER TO SWING AROUND INTO AN EDDY WHILE LYING ON HIS/HER BACK.

pendulum the swimmer into rocks, a hole or a strainer. (Obvious as it seems; this is a common mistake.)

■ Learn to repack or 'stack' the rope quickly and cleanly into its bag. Keep mud off the rope. Repacking is easier if you stand with your back to the trailing end and draw it over your shoulder.

Throwbagging the right way

DO

■ Learn to throw the bag in one of the ways illustrated below.

■ Shout 'Rope!' as you hurl the throwbag slightly downstream of the swimmer.

■ Always stand on the loose or 'dead' end of the rope while managing the coil or throwbag to avoid entanglement.

■ Position yourself above an eddy, in order to pendulum the swimmer into the bank. Do not

DO NOT

■ Knot the end of the rope, make a loop in it or knot it around the hand or wrist.

■ Put weights in the throwbag. (Use water instead.)

■ Stand downstream of the rope. Make sure that it pendulums away from you and does not sweep your legs from under you.

Roping follies

Ropework on rivers is specialized and ropes may be the biggest lifesaver in emergencies.

But in the wrong hands they are very hazardous as they become moving strainers.

In multiple rescue situations, it is clear that throwing ropes into rivers can result in a tangled mess, wrapping around the limbs or neck of anyone unlucky enough to swim into the thick of it. Ropes should be carefully targeted, quickly retrieved and rebagged or recoiled. Rope-throwers should never attempt to carry out multiple rescues in the same area.

Some mistakes a rescuer might make are to stand on a high rock, to wrap the rope around the wrist and not to wear a helmet and lifejacket.

Remember to always hold the end of the rope when you throw the bag to a swimmer. There is a grab loop at the bottom of the throwbag which the swimmer should get hold of, but he/she can also grab the rope itself or the whole throwbag.

THIS PRACTICE SESSION SHOWS DIFFERENT WAYS OF USING A THROWBAG STUFFED WITH ROPE. THROWING METHODS INCLUDE:

A UNDERHAND. B OVERHAND. C AS A TORPEDO. D A COILED ROPE THROWS BEST WITH THE SIDEWINDER METHOD.

Ropes and knots

Knots and Rope Types

Ropes are a necessary evil on rivers. Buy a good handbook on knots and knot tying, take the time to learn basic knot techniques and practise tying them.

Rafters use several kinds of ropes for different purposes:

■ Tie-ons for vehicles should be nylon or polyester. The trucker's hitch is used to tension them.

■ Tie-downs for rafts should be lighter polyprop lines or straps, cut to length. Burn the edges to avoid fraying.

■ Mooring lines to secure rafts are made of soft braid.

■ Rescue lines, stowed in throwbags or coiled as free-running lines, should float and be brightly coloured to be visible on the water.

■ Haul lines to pull boats free from wraps and pins are also used for rescue lines, and are made of heavy static (non-stretch) rope.

When coiling ropes (J), ensure that the successive loops are flat, and lie evenly on top of each other with no twists. At the end, wrap the 'live' end of the rope around the coil (K), loop it through the coil and tighten. Leave the end of the rope free as a tie-on (L).

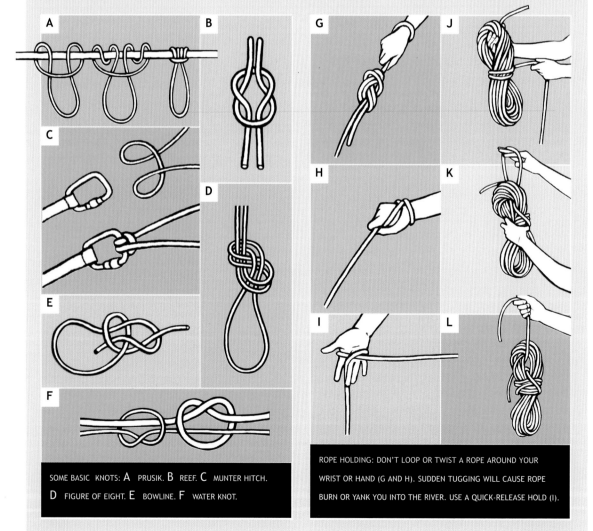

SOME BASIC KNOTS: A PRUSIK. B REEF. C MUNTER HITCH. D FIGURE OF EIGHT. E BOWLINE. F WATER KNOT.

ROPE HOLDING: DON'T LOOP OR TWIST A ROPE AROUND YOUR WRIST OR HAND (G AND H). SUDDEN TUGGING WILL CAUSE ROPE BURN OR YANK YOU INTO THE RIVER. USE A QUICK-RELEASE HOLD (I).

Swiftwater rescue techniques

Having an action plan

The chart on this page is not a replacement for good judgement. It maps out the typical rescue situations and suggests the action imperatives (AIs) — a rescuer's key concerns. The most important AI is always to keep the victim alive and motivated in the river before carrying out rescue. Motivation is very important because victims sometimes just give up, so communicate positively with them at all times.

Although one's natural instinct is to attempt instant rescue, a failed rescue wastes valuable time. The person who is the focus of a rescue attempt is known as the victim. A rescued person who requires first aid becomes a patient.

The action plan helps to structure your rescue approach around predictable scenarios.

■ **Hazards:** First, ascertain what hazards face the rescuers, the victims and the onlookers and take preventive action. For example, in a flood situation, get the onlookers onto safe ground.

■ **Four scenarios:** In a multiple rescue scenario, there are different logical follow-up plans. The victim/s may be stationary, moving away in the water, vanished, or all of these.

■ **Incident Command:** Rescue teams are most effective when there is co-ordination under a unified plan of action. The IC is often the first person on the scene that assumes command by default. If there is a safety officer, command should pass to him/her.

■ **Onlookers:** Bystanders often get in the way; more worryingly, they disappear and flee the river. Assign someone to keep them together and keep them informed on a regular basis.

■ **Watch your crew:** Urge them on and provide group support. After the rescue, hold an informal debriefing to allow them to voice their pent-up stress.

ACTION PLAN FOR RIVER RESCUE	
ASSESS	Analyze the situation before acting. Stay away from hazards yourself: ask 'What if?' should plans not work out. Avoid impulsive actions. Review your plan at intervals.
COMMUNICATE	The key to successful rescues is communication. If time allows, discuss the situation. Hand signals are mostly used to convey the plan and direct action strategies.
TEAM PLAN	For effective teamwork, set clear goals and keep in touch with each person. Discourage personal heroics and avoid undue risk to rescuers.
INCIDENT COMMAND	A single person should be in charge and visible to all. The Incident Commander (IC) can be the first experienced person on the scene who assumes control.
ONLOOKERS	Issue clear instructions to onlookers to remain together and stay out of the rescue unless asked to assist. Onlookers can get into trouble themselves. Watch them carefully!
NOTICE!	Stay alert, be flexible. Pay attention to the physical and mental state of everyone involved. Motivate all with positive signals. Call a halt or revise the action plan if necessary.

WHEN USING THROWBAGS OR THROWROPES TO PULL IN A SWIMMER DURING A RESCUE, PRACTISE ACCURACY AND LEARN TO RECOIL THE ROPE SPEEDILY.

A THROW THE BAG WITH A LONG, FOLLOW-THROUGH ACTION.

B SHOUT 'ROPE!' AND LET THE SWIMMER GRAB THE ROPE.

C LEAN BACKWARDS AND SWING THE SWIMMER INTO AN EDDY. REMEMBER TO WARN SWIMMERS TO STAY CALM.

Different rescue methods

People go on whitewater trips to run rapids, not to walk around them. However, if some get very nervous and prefer to avoid big rapids, they should not feel pressured by the group to risk their necks. To minimize mishaps, an Incident Commander takes charge and posts a rescue boat or boats and skilled throwbaggers at strategic points (see sequence above).

It is helpful to know the history of a rapid as this indicates where rescue is likely to be most necessary.

Strong swimmer rescue

In some situations — above a strainer or waterfall — it takes a swimmer to catch a swimmer. Obviously this is hazardous, but a rope provides safety.

■ **Swimmer's harness:** The rescuer (a strong swimmer) clips the rope into the quick-release harness on his rescue PFD. Others on the bank manage the rope as the rescuer leaps in.

■ **Frog jumping** (see diagram): Never dive into a river. If you must, for swim rescues, launch out flat and belly flop on the water. Rescuers may need to frog-jump in shallow, rocky areas where landing flat is imperative though bruises are still likely.

■ **Fend-off:** A panicking swimmer can drown both of you. Fend a frantic swimmer off with the forearm across the chest or the heel of the hand on the chin. Turn the swimmer around and lie on your backs — in effect, back-ferrying on the haul rope, with the current pushing you diagonally into the bank.

Wader rescue

Wading is a very common method of effecting a rescue assist or reaching a trapped person quickly. This is one instance where an experienced rescuer may break the rules, even though wading with the water above the knees poses the risk of foot entrapment in crevices or against ledges (see A on p71). Learning to wade properly in moving water and applying some basic rules is essential (see p71).

■ **Face upstream:** When crossing a boulder sieve, look at where the current is coming from, as well as

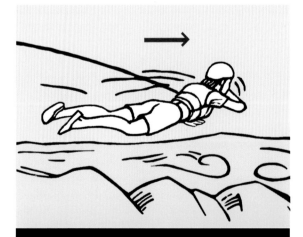

diagram IF YOU MUST THROW YOURSELF INTO THE WATER TO RESCUE SOMEONE, LAND AS FLAT AS POSSIBLE IN A KIND OF BELLY FLOP. AVOID SPLASHING DOWN HEAVILY AS THERE MAY BE ROCKS JUST BENEATH THE SURFACE OF THE WATER. TAKE CARE TO PROTECT YOUR BODY AND FACE BY SPREADING YOUR HANDS FACE DOWNWARDS.

where it is going. Lean upstream and use your hands under the water if necessary (B).

■ **Use the eddies:** Facing upstream allows you to see the eddies. Use them wherever possible as they break the force of the current.

■ **One foot at a time:** Feel around for a foothold, ascertaining that there is nothing to wedge you tight. Move one foot at a time (C).

■ **Lunge across channels:** When the current is too deep and strong, lunge forward and swim for the next available eddy.

■ **Safety line:** It is wise to be on a harness and safety line, especially if lives depend on your reaching the objective. If you slip, get hauled in and try again.

■ **Pole support:** Lean on a staunch tree branch or a paddle, using the grip as the foot (the blade will wobble in the current).

■ **Threesomes and twosomes:** Three people making a triangle can get a better foothold. Two pivot around as one stands with his or her back to the current. Two can also use this method.

■ **Wear shoes,** but be wary of straps and buckles on river sandals that often catch in rocks.

Trapped victims and strainers

The weight of water pushes an inert or struggling body onto obstacles and keeps it there. If you go rafting on a river with many strainers, one of the essential elements of the Safety Talk is to teach all crew members how to get over a strainer. It is also helpful to do some dry land practice.

As soon as you encounter a strainer, grab it and climb up out of the water, being careful not to get entangled. Not all strainers are trees; fences, bridges, car wrecks, boulder sieves, tree roots and reedbanks all form nasty strainers.

■ The AI is to secure victims so they cannot slip further underwater. This usually means stringing a rope from upstream and getting it under the arms.

■ The rescuer can walk onto the strainer, while being protected by a safety line on a harness, to attach a separate line, or the victim can be lassoed.

■ Rescue may entail hauling the victim upstream, clearing the strainer or cutting it away with saws.

■ Wherever possible, rescuers should approach the victims from above (it may, however, be necessary to climb down the tree or rope down from the bridge).

PRACTISE WADING IN WATER UNTIL YOU BECOME PROFICIENT. A WADING IN WATER ABOVE THE KNEES CAN RESULT IN FOOT ENTRAPMENT, SO FEEL CAREFULLY WITH YOUR FEET AND AVOID STEPPING INTO CREVICES. B WHEN CROSSING ROCKS, USE YOUR HANDS AND LEAN UPSTREAM. C ALWAYS MOVE IN BALANCE, ONE FOOT AT A TIME, AND SWIM ACROSS DEEP CHANNELS.

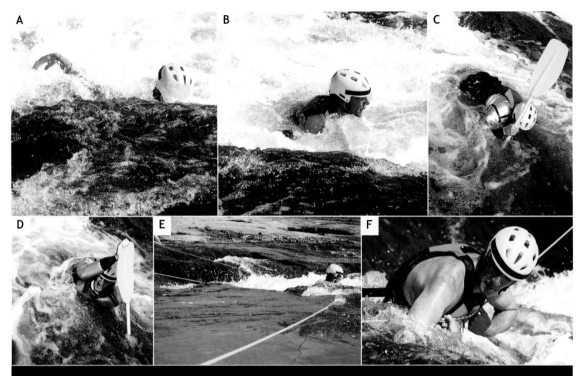

STABILIZATION OF FOOT-ENTRAPPED PERSON:

A PERSON WHO IS STUCK BETWEEN ROCKS MAY HAVE ONLY ONE LIMB ENTRAPPED OR COULD BE IN A FULL BODY PIN, WITH THE CURRENT FORCING HIM FURTHER INTO THE CREVICE ALL THE TIME. THIS PRACTICE SESSION DEMONSTRATES HOW TO STABILIZE AN ENTRAPPED PERSON SO HE CAN BREATHE. RESCUE FOLLOWS AFTERWARDS.

A THE VICTIM IS ENTRAPPED WITH HEAD UNDERWATER.

B THE VICTIM CAN LIFT HIS HEAD, BUT NOT EASILY.

C A PADDLE, POLE OR BRANCH IS THROWN TO THE VICTIM SO HE CAN LEAN ON IT TEMPORARILY.

D THE PADDLE BLADE IS UP AND THE HANDLE IS DOWN ON THE BOTTOM.

E ANOTHER ROPE IS STRETCHED ACROSS THE RIVER AND UNDER THE VICTIMS' ARMS.

F THE VICTIM CAN LEAN AGAINST THE SECOND ROPE (KNOWN AS A STABILIZATION LINE).

Foot entrapment

A person whose foot is caught in the rocks is likely to be in pain as the force of the current pushes them over, sometimes resulting in broken ankles and shin bones.

■ The Action Imperative (AI) of a foot-entrapped person is to help him/her stand upright and breathe.

■ In a typical sequence of an entrapment exercise (like the one shown above), the victim first receives a paddle to lean on temporarily. A branch or pole can also be used. Then a stabilization line is placed across the river to pull the victim to his feet. Once secured, rescue can begin.

■ Rescue may take place with a single swimmer or wader reaching the victim by coming down a separate line strung across the river. To avoid the victim's fate, the rescuer stays on the downstream side in the 'body eddy' formed by the victim.

■ If the rescue involves a team using ropes, it may be acceptable to approach from upstream. A raft is suspended in the current by rope managers upstream (it is attached on the other side to a log). Rope handlers can also use a tree for friction. A swimmer is lowered from the raft to reach the victim and manhandle him free.

Wraps and pins

A wrapped raft is not a disaster, unless somebody is pinned by the pressure of the raft against the rock.

Any boat can wrap — an oarboat, paddle raft, cataraft, inflatable or hard-hulled canoes or kayaks — and each one presents special difficulties.

■ **Large inflatable rafts** may require heavy-duty ropework to free them. For this, knowledge of mechanical advantage systems like vector pulls and z-drags is necessary.

■ **Smaller rafts** tend to puncture or deflate under a lot of water pressure, then wrap themselves very tightly around the obstacle.

■ **Hard-hulled boats** like dories and kayaks fill with water and can fold or break up.

Look after the passengers first, settle them down on the rock or send a boat to fetch them.

Unwrapping a raft is quite a science in itself. Try taking advantage of currents when setting up haul lines. A roll-over line pulls one end of the raft away from the rock, either lifting the upstream tube out of the water or flipping the raft so that it floats free. A downriver dragline pulls it on the side where the current is strongest.

Be careful when hauling, as tackle under great strain and friction can snap, catapulting broken carabiners and lashing ropes back towards the handlers. Always pull facing away from the maximum haul.

Pinning

Technically a pinning refers to a boat that is wedged nose or tail down in the river, possibly with someone inside. However, the term is generally used to describe a victim pinned by any kind of boat.

■ The AI is to help the victim to breathe. While setting up haul lines to release pressure, secure the victim with a safety line. Try wedging a paddle, dry bags or boxes between the boat and the rock to create some space.

■ Pinning rescue is the same as for entrapment, and entails releasing the victim once the pinning raft has been removed. The raft may have to be cut away — an expensive option, but life and limb come first.

■ The victim could be pinned underwater facing downstream, with a pocket of air in front of the face. This gives vital minutes but it is an AI emergency.

Keepers and weirs

The churning, growling, perpetual violence of a gnarly keeper hole is enough to chill the nerves of seasoned river rescuers. Keeper holes recycle swimmers like socks in a washing machine.

There are ways to get out successfully, as demonstrated by Swimmers A and B (See Diagram below). A has been thrown a line and is being dragged out sideways, along the slot, to open water. B swims to the bottom and allows the undertow to flush him through safely, past the boil line.

The swimmers at C and D will soon be exhausted. At C, the foam pile is highest, and the aerated water hardly allows the swimmer to reach the surface for a breath. D stands a chance of reaching the corner, or eye of the slot, but because this is a 'frowner', he will probably keep getting washed back to the middle.

■ The AI for swimmers in 'keepers' is to get them out.

■ Rescue entails reaching swimmers with a throwline or getting close enough to grab them. Rescue can also

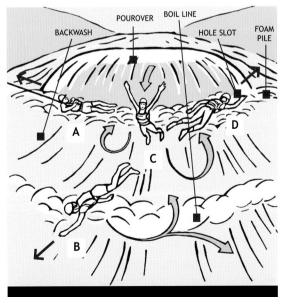

diagram THE SWIMMERS ABOVE DEMONSTRATE INEFFECTIVE AND SUCCESSFUL METHODS OF GETTING OUT OF A CHURNING KEEPER HOLE.

proceed with a raft on a stern line. The raft itself will be pulled into the backwash. Do not allow it to turn sideways, or it will flip swimmers into the foam pile.

■ A raft in a keeper could stay there a long time. A throwbag filled with stones or sand may be flung into the body of the raft as a grapple. Alternatively, get a rope across the river and walk it down both banks to snag it on or under the boat.

■ Finally, a rescue raft on a line may approach and the front man get hold of the raft's handline; one pull usually frees it.

Action that boaters should take to avoid a gnarly keeper hole:

■ If it's too late to avoid it, paddle strongly. Try to punch the foam pile and remember to keep paddling through the backwash.

■ Stay on the raft if possible. It will spin crazily and hurl people off, but it is a safety platform (of sorts), worth staying on until it flushes out of the hole of its own accord or dunks you in the water first.

Siphons

In engineering terms, a siphon is a tube that transfers liquid from one level to another under atmospheric pressure. In river terms it is a nasty underwater tunnel in the rocks (it could also be an actual pipe below a bridge or low-head dam).

What makes siphons particularly awful is they are often blocked by debris, forming an underwater strainer. The victim cannot be seen and may be trapped there until the river drops or a recovery unit removes all the debris (Diagram 1).

Siphons are not easily visible. An innocent swirl against a rockface may signal the bathplug action of a suck-down. Look for water erupting behind rocks. This is a sure sign that pressure has forced it through a submerged channel. You could also study the river at lower levels to see where siphons might form under tumbled boulders.

■ The AI for any victim in a siphon is to try to pull them back or carefully pull them through — if they can be reached at all.

Disappearance: Group search

There are many reasons why people go missing on trips. Some hike off to see the view, while others go for a swim. More seriously, people get into trouble in the river, get lost at night or fall down cliffs. These situations could be an emergency, leading to a group search, while serious disappearances would result in the need for air or ground searches by external Search and Rescue teams.

■ To avoid unnecessary panic, tell people to remain with the group at all times. If they do leave, the leader or deputy must always be informed and give their consent.

■ Unless trip leaders count heads at every stop, it is quite possible for someone to disappear from the party and not be noticed until much later.

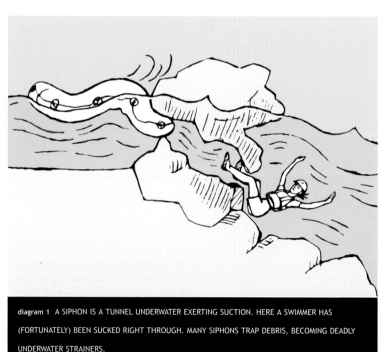

diagram 1 A SIPHON IS A TUNNEL UNDERWATER EXERTING SUCTION. HERE A SWIMMER HAS (FORTUNATELY) BEEN SUCKED RIGHT THROUGH. MANY SIPHONS TRAP DEBRIS, BECOMING DEADLY UNDERWATER STRAINERS.

■ Prevent disappearances by having a 'buddy' system — where people are teamed up in pairs at the beginning of the trip and told to watch each other.

■ **Where last seen:** Replay the last sighting of the person, from all witnesses.

■ **If in the river:** The person has either been washed out of sight or is in or under the water. Begin by using a logical process of elimination of all moving and stationary possibilities.

■ **If on land:** Study the terrain to estimate time and distance from present location. Investigate the most likely pathways.

■ **If unknown:** The problem expands to include all possibilities, and means having to spread your search team members rather thinly.

Searchers must go in pairs and the IC needs to set a time and place for rendezvous: no more than an hour in most cases. Searchers should have maps or notebooks to sketch maps, along with water and small first aid kits to deal with emergencies.

If a person has not been found after six to eight hours, the feasibility of an external Search and Rescue scenario should be considered.

Multiple Rescues

In principle, multiple rescues are like any other situation: but with more people in trouble they place a great strain on group's resources, making single Incident Command difficult, if not impossible. In this scenario, it becomes essential to prioritize the rescue effort to focus on situations that are life-threatening.

■ A person with a broken limb, but safe on the bank, can be given comfort by an onlooker until first aid is rendered.

■ A person stuck in a strainer in mid-river must be extricated quickly.

■ A disappeared person is not such an immediate problem unless you know his or her whereabouts under the water, in which case there will be two extreme emergencies.

■ Divide the command and deal with each emergency separately, if you can. Otherwise concentrate on the person most likely to survive.

COMMUNICATION CAN BECOME DIFFICULT IN A MULTIPLE RESCUE. THIS IS WHEN PRIORITIZING EACH EMERGENCY SEPARATELY CAN MINIMIZE PROBLEMS.

A few simple guidelines should apply to whitewater first aid:

■ Have a complete first aid kit in a waterproof ammo can or O-ring plastic case. It should be painted white with a red cross, be visible and accessible on the leading raft and be secured against capsizes. The box should also contain a manual on wilderness first aid. (See p 91 for a first aid kit list).

■ Learn the emergency procedures chart opposite as a mental map of procedures for a patient emergency. **Apart from drowning, you should be equipped to treat these typical river-related injuries and illnesses.**

■ Hypothermia is a life-threatening condition. It can happen anywhere, but mostly occurs in cold climates.

■ Heat stroke is an emergency. Heat exhaustion is a less serious condition.

■ Neck and spinal injuries may be sustained while swimming down rapids.

■ Severe bleeding may occur from the same causes, or from campsite and hiking accidents.

■ A range of infections, bites, digestive and bowel problems, colds, and minor discomforts are due to paddling, such as tendonitis.

■ Communication becomes the biggest problem in multiple rescues. Rescuers become spread out, time elapses, and ignorance of the situation breeds panic in the group, with dissent likely to follow. Put the group under a responsible marshal charged with getting them to safety and comfort. Once a rescue has been handled, provide information about it to all concerned and move on to the next one.

First Aid Emergencies

First aid means giving immediate and basic care to someone in distress or in a life-threatening situation. First aid should therefore be seem as vital aid. Well-trained first aid people can relieve pain and make the difference between life and death. Wilderness first aid relates to dealing with personal injuries in places that are geographically remote. The importance of first aid rises in direct proportion to the distance and time away from 'civilized' facilities. Ambulances and clinics are nowhere close by, so assessment and treatment must take place in the outdoors. If the injury is serious enough the patient will have to be evacuated before full medical care can be obtained.

■ Being properly qualified and certified in first aid is certainly a prerequisite for anyone leading or doing rescues on a whitewater trip. Do a first aid course under an acknowledged authority such as Red Cross or St John's Ambulance.

■ Commercial operators have a duty of care to employ guides with up-to-date qualifications (but check just in case). The situation with private trips is not as clear-cut since no-one may be ultimately responsible for group safety; so ensure that some people on the trip are qualified, ideally those who will be doing rescues.

External help and Casevac

A major problem in getting external help is trying to communicate your needs to the local emergency response services. Cellphones and two-way radios do not work well in river valleys, if they work at all, unless you can establish line-of-sight with a radio mast. This usually means that a pair of people from the group will have to hike out or run downriver in a boat to get help.

To call for help from external sources is a serious decision that will probably put an end to your rafting trip if that has not already happened.

Discuss with the group whether this action is really necessary, and whether the delay is going to make things better or worse.

Bear in mind that in developed regions, emergency teams are usually equipped and prepared for outdoor rescues, but elsewhere it may be the military or commercial services that respond, if anyone. This should be ascertained in advance of the trip.

Search and Rescue can involve a large operation and is not undertaken lightly by the authorities. Casualty evacuation (Casevac) is usually a small-scale affair, however you could be charged for it, so remember to make provision for this in your insurance cover.

Noting, recording, reporting

Callous as it may seem in the midst of a rescue, taking photographs and making notes does help at a later stage to ensure correct reporting, analysis of the accident site and assistance in possible legal or insurance claims that may arise.

■ **Correct reporting:** Incident reports are required by most commercial operators and are sometimes mandatory legal procedures. A video camera with date and time on the picture is an invaluable aid to ensure accuracy and recall.

■ **Accident site analysis:** Your own group and other river-runners will benefit and can learn from their mistakes by replaying the scene. Draw a map of it.

■ **Legal and insurance:** Evidence is undoubtedly a two-edged sword, but it is better to have it than not to have it. Anyone giving expert testimony on events could use the notes and photos, even if a court does not accept them as evidence.

When getting external help remember:

■ Always send written details. Include the date and time of the accident, the nature of the problem, map references or approximate location by noticeable landmarks, as well as the names and home contact details of the ill or injured persons.

■ Helicopter pilots find it difficult to land in confined river valleys, and prefer open grassy patches on hilltops. This could mean having to carry your casualty over rough terrain. Carry and strap the patient onto a stretcher or a makeshift bodyboard to prevent a fall.

■ Find a suitable landing zone (LZ), mark it with a large X with colourful groundsheets or clothing, and use a mirror to attract attention.

■ Do not expect helicopter pilots to fly at night, or vehicle drivers to find you easily in trackless country. Your group could be on its own for hours or even days before help arrives.

EMERGENCY PROCEDURES CHART

1. Taking stock

HELLO
Establish whether the person is conscious. If so, ask about injuries.

HEAD TO TOE
Inspect the patient fully to decide what IMMEDIATE action to take.

HAZARD
Remove the patient, yourself and onlookers from further dangers, if possible.

HELP
Call for help from others, and if necessary send for help from outsiders.

2. Primary survey - keep checking the systems!

AIRWAY
Look, listen and feel for signs of breathing. If there is water in the airway, turn the patient carefully, protecting the neck, to drain the water.

Respiratory System

BREATHING
Airway is open but breathing is non-existent or shallow. Begin artificial respiration.

CIRCULATION
■ **PULSE:** Airway is open but there is no pulse: the heart has stopped. Begin CPR.
■ **BLEEDING:** Stop any major loss of blood. Place pressure on the wound with the hand or a cloth.

Circulatory System

DISABILITY
Be aware that injuries to the nervous system (e.g. neck break) can cause paralysis or mental abnormalities.

Nervous System

EMOTION
Communicate with the patient and care-givers to lessen shock.

3. Heart & lungs

CARDIO PULMONARY RESUSCITATION
Lifesaving treatment must begin if the patient has no pulse and is unresponsive. Lifesaving means ventilating the patient air and restarting the blood flow.

REMEMBER TO USE:
■ Mouthpieces, to avoid contact with infectious diseases, mainly hepatitis.
■ Surgical gloves, to avoid contact with blood (risk of Aids).
■ Airways tubes (different sizes) to keep the patient's airway open if necessary.

Rafting Today

World whitewater routes
Finding out

Rafting trips are run on thousands of great rivers throughout the world, with some exciting new destinations in Africa, Asia and the East. Organized trips are available on most. For information regarding permits which may be needed for private trips through nature reserves or military regions contact the International Rafting Federation. This lists national rafting associations where they exist, and also tourism bodies for each country or region. Search the Internet (i.e. websites such as Find a Guide) for details of major river operators in different parts of the world. Since details can change, it's important to have updated information about what to bring, medical warnings, as well as organized trip schedules and prices.

■ **International Rafting Federation:**
http://www.intraftfed.com/
■ **Find A Guide: www.findaguide.com/raft.htm**

WHITEWATER RATING GUIDE

RELAXING trips cover mainly flat water with few rapids and are not included in this book. Rapids are Class 1 & 2, suitable for people of all ages, including the unfit and non-swimmers.

MODERATE trips include Class 2 & 3 rafting and are suitable for any person in reasonably good physical condition with no experience. Short hikes and sudden swims are likely.

FAIRLY STRENUOUS trips are physically tiring. Expect to walk along river banks and swim through wild rapids after falling out. Rapids of Class 3 & 4. Previous rafting experience is not vital but participants should be self-reliant.

VERY STRENUOUS trips are physically extremely tough and demanding. Participants will need to have a high level of fitness and be able to portage loads, hike in rugged terrain and swim strongly in rough water. As the rapids may reach Grade 5, leaders and companions will probably expect participants on these trips to have rafting experience.

Listing format

- ■ REGION OF THE WORLD
- ■ RIVER (overall grading in brackets)
- ■ Country
- ■ Closest city or major town
- ■ Recommended river craft
- ■ Grading of most difficult rafted sections
- ■ Duration of trip
- ■ Season of the year
- ■ What to expect
- ■ Tourism body website address
- ■ Tourism e-mail contacts
- ■ Recommended operators

Key to recommended craft

RR	= Raft rig (oar/motorized)
OB	= Oarboat
DY	= Dory
PR	= Paddle raft
SO	= Small oarboat (e.g. cataraft)
IK	= Inflatable kayak/canoe
HY	= Hydrospeed & boards
HC	= Hard-hulled kayak/canoe

opposite page RAFTERS CHALLENGE THE TEETH-GRITTING RAPIDS OF THE KARAMEA RIVER ON THE SOUTH ISLAND OF NEW ZEALAND.

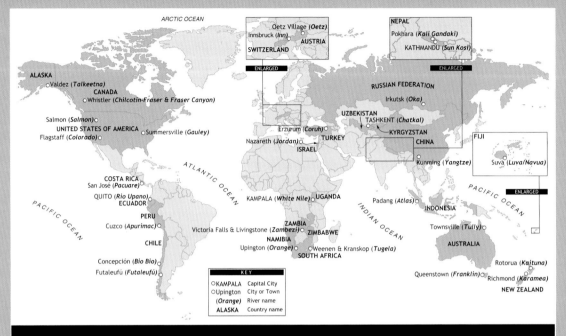

KEY

○KAMPALA Capital City
○Upington City or Town
(*Orange*) River name
ALASKA Country name

USE THE WORLD MAP TO LOCATE THE REGION AND THE RIVER.

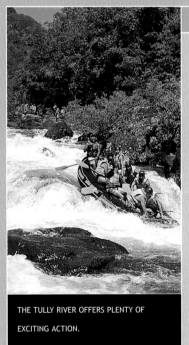

THE TULLY RIVER OFFERS PLENTY OF
EXCITING ACTION.

AUSTRALIA

FRANKLIN (moderate 3)

- Tasmania State
- Queenstown
- (Paddle craft) PR, SO, IK, HY, KC
- Class 5
- 8 – 14 days
- November – March
- Tea-coloured rapids, stained by vegetation, boil between ravines surrounded by temperate forests.
- www.tourism.tas.gov.au
- Use same site for e-mail
- Tasmanian Wild River Adventures; World Expeditions.

TULLY (fairly strenuous 3 – 4)

- Queensland State
- Townsville
- (Paddle craft) PR, SO, IK, KC
- Class 4
- 5 hours
- All year
- Not a big-volume river, the Tully has a reputation for big action, with more than 45 rapids in a morning's run, including Alarm Clock Falls and Wet 'n Moisty.
- http://aussie.net.au
- qttcinfo@qttc.com.au
- Raging Thunder; Raft 'n Rainforest.

AFRICA

WHITE NILE (fairly strenuous 3 — 4)
- Uganda ■ Kampala
- (All craft) OB, PR, SO, IK, KC
- Class 5
- 1 — 2 days
- All year
- The Victoria Nile below the Owen Falls is 3 — 6 times the volume of the Zambezi and is equally clean and wild. It offers trips of a day or more. The proposed Bujagali Dam threatens the main whitewater stretch of the river.
www.visituganda.com
- utb@starcom.co.ug
- Adrift; Nile Explorers; Unusual Destinations.

ZAMBEZI (fairly strenuous 3 — 4)
- Zimbabwe; Zambia
- Victoria Falls; Livingstone
- (All craft) OB, PR, SO, IK, HY, KC
- Class 4
- 1 — 6 days
- August — December (low water) and January — March (high water)
- This is one of the greatest high-adrenaline trips on water.
- Zimbabwe: www.zimbabwe.net/tourism
- Zambia: www.africa-insites.com/zambia
- Zimbabwe: tventure@icon.co.zw
- Zambia: zntb@zamnet.zm
- Shearwater; Safari Par Excellence; Frontiers.

TUGELA (fairly strenuous 3 — 4)
- South Africa
- Weenen and Kranzkop
- (Paddle craft) PR, SO, IK, KC
- Class 4
- 1 — 8 days
- November — March
- The Tugela (meaning 'the one that startles') includes rapids such as Rocky Horror, Horrible Horace and Four Man Hole.
- www.tourism-kzn.org
- info@tourism-kzn.org
- Zingela Safaris; River Tours and Safaris.

ORANGE (Gariep)
(fairly strenuous 2 — 4)
- South Africa/Namibia
- Upington, Northern Cape
- (Paddle craft) PR, SO, IK, HY, KC
- Class 5
- 2 — 4 days
- All year
- The generally placid Orange River turns wild in the Kalahari Desert. Both the Augrabies Falls and Gariep Falls are approached and followed by numerous rapids.
- www.wcapetourism.co.za
- www.travelsa.com/provincp.html
- travel@rapidttp.com
- Gravity Tours; Intrapid; River Rafters.

PACIFIC AND EAST

ATLAS (moderate 3 — 4)
- Sumatra, Indonesia ■ Padang
- (Paddle craft) PR, SO, IK, KC
- Class 4
- 1 — 3 days
- All year
- Indonesia contains over 13,000 fertile volcanic islands with many rivers. In the Gunung Leuser Reserve, the powerful river Atlas squeezes through deep ravines where portaging is sometimes necessary.
- www.tourismindonesia. com/advent.htm
- nusa@indobiz.com
- Contact national rafting association through IRF.

LUVA and NAVUA
(relaxing 2 — 3)
- Fiji ■ Nadi or Suva
- (Small craft) SO, IK, HY, KC
- Class 3
- 1 day
- All year
- Journey through the rainforest of the Namori highlands, which takes you to the Wainikoroiluva (Luva) River. Fun rapids skirt rock mazes and cascades.
- www.fiji.gov.fj/m-tourism
- www.fijiislands.org
- rob@fijiguide.com
- Rivers Fiji.

ASIA

SUN KOSI (moderate 3 — 4)

- Nepal
- Kathmandu
- (Paddle craft) PR, SO, IK, KC
- Class 5
- 1 — 10 days
- March — May, October — December.
- The 'River of Gold' with its big warm-water rapids cuts through the Himalayas on its journey through Nepal to join the Ganges in Northern India.
- www.welcomenepal.com info@ntb.wlink.com.np
- Adrift; Ultimate Descents; Team Gorky Adventure Travel.

KALI GANDAKI

(fairly strenuous 3 — 4)

- Nepal ■ Pokhara
- (Paddle craft) PR, SO, IK,KC
- Class 5
- 3 days or up to 10 days
- March — May, October — December.
- The Kali carves the deepest gorge in the world between the Dhaulagiri and Annapurna peaks which are 8000m (26,000ft-plus) high.
- www.visitnepal.com
- ecotreks@getaway.mos.com.np
- Ultimate Descents; Himalayan Eco Treks; Equator Expeditions; Whitewater Voyages.

CHATKAL RIVER (fairly strenuous 4)

- Russia, Kyrgyzstan & Uzbekistan
- Tashkent
- (Paddle craft) PR, SO, IK, KC
- Class 4
- 5 days
- July — September
- Fed by glaciers, this river flows through relatively dry country with scenic peaks all around and has been described by river-runners as 'a river made in heaven'.
- www.russia.tourism.run
- info@russia.tourism.ru
- See IRF contacts.

YANGTZE (fairly strenuous 4)

- China
- Kunming
- (Paddle craft) PR, SO, IK, KC
- Class 5
- 9 — 15 days
- February — March, August —October
- The high Yangtze in the Kunlun Mountains of Tibet and the upper Yangtze's Great Bend are expeditionary challenges.
- www.chinats.com
- bisc@chinats.com
- High Asia; Earth River Expeditions.

AN IMPRESSIVE HIGHLIGHT OF THE YANGTZE IS FLOATING THE GREAT BEND, AND HIKING THROUGH THE TIGER LEAPING GORGE.

SAYAN OKA RIVER

(moderate 3 — 4)

- Irkutsk
- (Paddle craft)OB, PR, SO, IK, KC
- Class 4+ ■ 4 — 12 days
- June — September
- With more than 53,000 rivers in Siberia, it is hard to choose just one. The Oka River in the Sayan Mountains near the border with Mongolia is a Siberian gem: big water with big-hearted guides.
- http://www.raft.org/russia/
- sierraoc@jps.net; travel@irk.ru
- Sierra Outdoor Centre; Baikal Rafting.

NORTH AMERICA

COLORADO (Grand Canyon)
(fairly strenuous 2 – 4)
- Arizona, USA
- Flagstaff ■ (All craft)
RR, OB, DY, PR, SO, IK, HY, KC
- Class 5
- 2 – 20 days ■ All year
- The Grand Canyon offers a range of rapids from easy to high-grade. Inquire about popular commercial routes 1 – 2 years in advance, and for private trips get onto the National Parks Service waiting list (up to 12 years).
- www.thecanyon.com/nps/ or www.grandcanyoninformation.com/raft
- info@canyon.net
- Numerous: see website above.

GAULEY (fairly strenuous 3 – 5)
- West Virginia, USA
- Summersville
- (All craft) RR, OB, DY, PR, SO, IK, KC
- Class 5 ■ 1 – 2 days
- September – October (high water)
- Fabulous rafting on several class rapids is possible for a month each fall when water is released from the Summersville Dam.
- www.nps.gov/gari or www.state.wv.us
- www.nps.gov/pub_aff/e-mail/ or ask-npf@nationalparks.org
- Ace Adventure Centre; Songer Whitewater; Class 6 River Runners; Mountain River Tours.

IDAHO – SALMON
(moderate 3 – 4)
- Idaho, USA ■ Salmon
- (Paddle craft) PR, SO, IK, KC
- Class 4
- 3 – 6 days ■ June – September
- The longest undammed river in the Lower 48 States, the Salmon has warm water, awesome scenery and rapids with names like Roller Coaster, Whiplash and Slide.
- www.travelidaho.com or
- http://www.visitid.org/outdoor/rivers/index.html
- rjust@idpr.state.id.us or ioga@ioga.org
- River Odysseys West (ROW); Middle Fork River Tours; Main Salmon: Lewis and Clark Trail Adventures.

TALKEETNA (moderate 3)
- Alaska, USA ■ Valdez
- (Paddle craft) PR, SO, IK, KC
- Class 4
- 4 – 5 days
- July – September
- The glacier-fed river is in pristine condition, churning green and white through beautiful wilderness with abundant wildlife.
- www.travelalaska.com
- ava@alaskanet.com
- Keystone Raft and Kayak Adventures; Earth River Expeditions.

RAFTERS PREPARE FOR A TRIP ON THE CATARACT CANYON OF THE COLORADO RIVER, KNOWN AS THE 'BIG DADDY' OF WHITEWATER.

CHILCOTIN – FRASER and FRASER CANYON (moderate 2 – 4)
- British Columbia, Canada
- Whistler
- (Large craft) RR, OB, DY, PR
- Class 4
- Canyon – 1 day; up to 6 days
- May – August
- The massive Fraser starts in the Canadian Rockies and flows to the Pacific. Volcanic canyons hem the river in, leading to the narrows of Hell's Gate Gorge.
- www.tbc.gov.bc.ca
- dbc@bc.sympatico.ca
- Canadian River Expeditions.

SOUTH AMERICA

RIO UPANO (fairly strenuous 3 — 4)

- Ecuador ■ Quito
- (Paddle craft) PR, SO, IK, HY, KC
- Class 3
- 6 days
- November — February
- Flowing through the mountainous Morona — Santiago province, this Amazon headwater starts in snow-covered volcanic slopes and descends into lush forest. Its hefty rapids are not too technical and suitable for fit people of any age.
- www.exploringecuador.com
- info@exploringecuador.com
- North by North West Adventure Travel; Remote Odysseys Worldwide.

BIO BIO (fairly strenuous 3 — 4)

- Chile ■ Victoria
- (Paddle craft) OB, PR, SO, IK, KC
- Class 4
- 1 — 14 days
- All year
- Bursting out of the Andes, the glacier-fed Bio Bio churns past ice cliffs and waterfalls in volcanic foothills. Trips vary greatly in length and can include hiking to native villages and bathing in hot springs.
- www.chileweb.net
- info@chileweb.net
- Earth River Expeditions; Mountain-Travel Sobek; Chris Spelius Expeditions.

PACUARE (very strenuous 4 — 5)

- Costa Rica ■ San José
- (Paddle craft) PR, SO, IK, HY, KC
- Class 5
- June to February
- 1 — 2 days
- The longest and most scenic of Costa Rica's rivers, the Pacuare is also its most exciting whitewater run, featuring amazing wildlife. The main section offers tense pool-and-drop rapids. An upper section offers extreme rafting for inflatable kayaks.
- www.tourism-costarica.com
- Contact via same site
- Rios Tropicalos; Ticos River Adventures.

APURIMAC (fairly strenuous 3 — 5)

- Peru ■ Cuzco
- (Paddle craft) PR, SO, IK, KC
- Class 5
- 3 — 4 days
- May — November
- Hike down from the Andes, 3400m (11,100ft) to 2000m (6550ft) above sea level, from where rafting begins on the most direct source of the Amazon. The rapids are feisty and the wildlife abundant.
- www.perutourism.com
- peru@perutourism.com
- Apurimac Rafting.

FUTALEUFÚ (fairly strenuous 3 — 5)

- Chile ■ Futaleufú
- (Paddle craft) PR, SO, IK, KC
- Class 5
- November — April
- In Patagonian Chile, the pristine Fu ranges between Class 5 rapids, fun-filled Class 3 play spots and tranquil stretches of flat water where you can see the bottom. World rafting championships were held on this river at the turn of the millennium.
- www.chileweb.net
- info@chileweb.net
- Nantahala Outdoor Centre; Earth River Expeditions; Neharot.

SPECTACULAR SCENERY IS A FEATURE OF CHILE'S FUTALEUFÚ RIVER.

EUROPE/MIDDLE EAST

INN (moderate 3)
- Switzerland, Austria
- Innsbruck
- (Paddle craft) PR, SO, IK, HY, KC
- Class 5
- 1 day
- May — September
- High up in the Engadin valley of Switzerland, the Inn offers serious whitewater with joyous rapids that are deep and quite easy.
- www.austria-tourism.at
- oeinfo@oewwien.via.at
- Ultimate Alps; Rafting Tours Augsburg.

OETZ RIVER (very strenuous 2 — 5)
- Austria, Tyrol ■ Oetz village
- PR, SO, KC
- Class 5
- 1.5 hours
- June — August
- A very turbulent Alpine torrent, not for the faint-hearted. Because the Oetz is a challenging high-grade river, participants are required to run the classic Inn River (graded 2 — 4) beforehand.
- Oetz tourism: search on www.tiscover.com
- Oetz tourism: tvb.oetz.@netway.at
- Rafting: RTAugsburg@AOL.com
- Rafting Tours Augsburg; Rios Tropicales.

CORUH (moderate 3 — 4)
- Turkey
- Erzurum
- (Paddle craft) PR, SO, IK, KC
- Class 5
- 4 — 8 days
- May — July
- This offers varied and exciting whitewater in the rugged and remote Kackar Mountains.
- www.turkey.org
- turkish@erols.com
- Adrift; Nantahala Outdoor Center; Alternatifraft.

JORDAN (moderate 2 — 3)
- Israel
- Nazareth
- (Paddle craft) PR, SO, IK, KC
- Class 3
- 2 hours to 1 day
- All year
- For a country not really considered a rafting destination, the Jordan in Northern Israel offers steep rapids as it plunges into the sea of Galilee.
- www.goisrael.com
- www.rafting.co.il
- Jordan River Rafting.

NEW ZEALAND

KAITUNA (fairly strenuous 4)
- North Island
- Rotorua
- (Paddle craft) PR, SO, IK, KC
- Class 5
- 1 hour
- All year
- In 45 minutes there are 14 drops including what is claimed to be the highest commercially run waterfall in the world, an exhilarating 7m (23ft).
- www.nztb.govt.nz
- Use internet site http://www.purenz.com/Feedback.cfm
- Kaituna Cascades; The Rush.

KARAMEA (fairly strenuous 4)
- South Island
- Richmond
- (Paddle craft) PR, SO, IK, KC
- Class 5
- 1 — 3 days
- October — April
- A teeth-gritting run down the river that roars, winding through the Kahurangi National Park in the shadow of Mount Cobb. Famed rapids include Roaring Lion and Scare-Case.
- www.nztb.govt.nz
- Use Internet site: http://www.purenz.com/Feedback.cfm
- Australian and Amazonian Adventures; Ultimate Descents.

THESE FUTURE RIVER-RUNNERS ON THE MARSAYANGDI RIVER IN NEPAL KNOW THE IMPORTANCE OF WEARING SAFETY EQUIPMENT FROM AN EARLY AGE, EVEN WHEN RAFTING ON MILD WATER.

A universal sport

Rafting has a media image as a male macho sport. The reality is that people of both sexes, all races and all ages go in for it. More recently, whitewater rafting adventures are being offered for special groups such as the physically disabled, the blind and those without the use of all their limbs.

A new trend is towards children's rafting trips. Rafters as young as six experience mild whitewater, while learning about turtles and snakes, how to reduce waste and solar energy as alternatives to damming.

The presence of women's teams and black paddlers in the world championships is a sign that competitive international whitewater rafting is no longer only dominated by white males. Although women have fitted into the world of professional rafting without controversy, many hold strong feelings about their role in the outdoors. Women, with a body mass on average some 20% less than that of men, rely more on technical skills and co-ordination to get down rapids. They show finesse in dealing with situations because they try harder to communicate — an all-important principle of river safety. Black adventurers are also coming into rafting in increasing numbers. Meanwhile, in Asia, Melanesia, the Pacific islands, and South America, local people are exploring their own rivers and offering rafting trips to visitors. They enrich any trip with their knowledge of lore and customs associated with rivers.

Legal and insurance issues

Mention the law and the eyes of most river-runners will glaze over. Yet legal issues crop up on rivers all the time. For sheer self-protection it is best to know your legal rights and what the law requires of you.

Legal systems differ markedly in different parts of the world. Certain principles, however, apply fairly generally. The main issues are access to rivers, your rights when booking a trip, and claims for accidents.

Adventure insurance packages should include:

■ Costs of search and rescue, evacuation and immediate medical treatment or hospitalization. Helicopter or aircraft Casevac with paramedical support on board is widely available in developed countries and may be obtainable, at a special premium, in other areas.

■ Payment is made in the event of death or permanent disability. This would also cover body repatriation and funeral costs.

■ The organizers of a trip may take out public liability insurance that covers for claims arising out of injury, loss or damage occurring in the course of a trip.

Legal responsibility
Inherent risk

Common law recognizes that whitewater rafting, like mountaineering and many other sports, involves inherent risks. Participants therefore may have no claim for injuries or losses arising from the activity itself. A claim will only be successful in cases where an organizer or leader is clearly negligent, or where the fault is caused by their own direct action (such as dropping your camera in the water).

Waivers and indemnities

All operators and most clubs will present you with a legal waiver or indemnity form to be signed before the trip. This is your agreement to undertake the trip at your own risk, and releases them from liability. If you refuse to sign, they may refuse to take you.

Some forms will state that there can be no claim even where the leaders are negligent or careless. But even when signed by you, a waiver may be challenged because your financial dependants (family, business associates) cannot have their rights signed away. Make sure you read the waiver very carefully before you abdicate your rights.

Strategies for access

Given the haziness and complexity of river accessing, consider these strategies:

■ Get in and out only at bridges or public parks.

■ When camping or crossing land, get the permission of the landowners.

■ Obtain letters of permission from government and especially from the military in their areas.

■ Obtain permits where necessary (if entering a conserved area or zone supervised by a large company).

River access

To avoid being arrested or sued, river-runners need to know their rights on a river.

Adjacent landowners often regard the river as their own, and can get very nasty with those they see as intruders. Be polite, but know your rights. Full ownership of the river by landowners is rare anywhere.

To establish the legal situation, find out:

1. How is the 'river' defined? It is usually regarded as the water in the channel. This varies from day to day.

2. What are the 'banks'? The 50 or 100-year high-water mark usually defines the channel, so the banks extend from the water to the high-water mark.

3. What is the 'riverbed'? This extends from the banks under the river and usually includes the rocks in the middle of the channel. Adjoining landowners may own the riverbed to the midpoint, so to get off the water and onto dry land or rocks could be trespassing.

4. Who 'owns' the river itself? The water may be owned by the State, a regional authority, a concession-holder, or even by the landowners.

Rights of access to the water are influenced by different legal traditions. These include:

■ **European law**, dating back to the Romans, tends to recognize rivers as public highways to which everyone has a right of access up to the high-water mark.

■ **British law** allows the surface of rivers to be privately controlled and therefore sold or rented, preventing access or boating if the owner refuses it.

■ **American law** mixes elements of both European and British law, depending on the individual State and its specific case judgements.

■ **Indigenous or tribal custom** in many countries treats rivers as communal property. To use them, one needs the permission of a chieftain or local authority.

■ **Military control** sweeps civilian law away. Rivers on conflicted borders are either ruled by the military, by terrorists, or by nobody. River access is risky and survival dubious.

Waterwise

'We were promised the adventure of a lifetime. We just didn't want it to be the last adventure of a lifetime.'
— Tim Cahill *(Outside Magazine)*

adventure on a rafting trip can so easily turn into misadventure. Having a sixth sense for the factors that can turn a journey into an ordeal is part of the river-runner's armoury of skills that inevitably develop with 'river time'.

Travel and personal security

With expeditions to foreign countries becoming the norm, safety issues extend well beyond the river itself. Crime is prevalent at many airports, bribery is endemic in certain official cultures, and overcharging is to be expected if you look wealthy. If you are intent on visiting a dangerous area, try to limit the risks to manageable river situations.

Heed these useful tips:

■ Obtain as much information as possible about the area beforehand by consulting the US State Department and other national travel advisory services. These are usually freely available over the Internet to all travellers (see contacts).

■ Get letters of introduction from as many officials or influential people as possible, and store copies of all important documentation in a safe depot.

■ Use a phrase book to learn some basic phrases in the local language so you can be minimally polite.

■ Do not discuss the details of your arrival, transport routes, equipment and stores with strangers.

■ Do not discuss politics and do show respect for soldiers. Always maintain your innocence, smile, and try to ensure there are witnesses when dealing with difficult or corrupt officials.

Water quality and purification

To drink unpurified river water or use it for dish cleaning is asking for trouble. No matter how clear it looks, river water always contains bacteria and often chemical pollutants as well. To lower the risk of infection or poisoning, every effort must be made to ensure that the water used is sterile.

Stomach upsets and skin rashes can be avoided with a few simple procedures. These days, water-purifying filters are widely available. Boiling the water also helps, as do substances, known as flocculents, that precipitate dissolved solids out of the water.

There are three classes of contaminants:

■ **Microbiological**, such as *E. coli* bacteria from animal faeces, various viruses and spores or parasites that carry diseases. The latter include the cold-water nasties, giardia and cryptosporidium, and the tropical flatworm bilharzia (or schistosomiasis).

■ **Chemical**, including pesticides, herbicides and fertilizers; metals such as lead; industrial waste and even natural substances from the rocks or vegetation which may cause illness.

■ **Aesthetic** refers to the muddy, smelly quality of some rivers that may not really be harmful, but certainly seems repugnant.

A solution may be to carry as much tap water as possible from home. On a multiday trip you have no option but to depend on drawing all water from the river for drinking, cooking and cleaning.

opposite page CLEAR RIVER WATER, LIKE THIS FOUND IN THE KARAMEA RIVER ON THE SOUTH ISLAND OF NEW ZEALAND, MAY LOOK DRINKABLE BUT MAY NOT BE SAFE. ALWAYS PURIFY WATER BEFORE DRINKING IT.

There are six options, taken singly or together, that should remove virtually all contaminants. Remember that common sense is the best defence!

■ Collect the water from midstream, not stagnant pools. Oxygenated water (from rapids) or that which has flowed through reedbeds tends to be fairly clean. Water from ground springs is usually the safest, although parasites may still lurk there.

■ Boiling at a full rolling boil for a minimum of 10 minutes will kill bacteria and parasites. Left to cool, a pot of boiled water will tend to clarify better than water merely left to stand. Decant the boiled water into clean containers.

■ Flocculate the water with alum powder or aluminium polycholoride. The flocculent attracts molecules of dissolved solids to itself, and the clarified water can once again be decanted into a clean container leaving discoloured foam behind.

■ Treat chemically, lacing each container of water that you gather with iodine, chlorine or household bleach. This will destroy many of the bacteria in the water (although not giardia). However, it requires time and the right dosage to work, and is slower in cold water.

■ Filter water using a purifier. Carbon filters remove unpleasant tastes (like iodine). Ceramic or polyethylene filters provide microfiltration down to a rating of .3 microns or smaller to eliminate microbiotic life.

■ Finally, cover the purified water and keep away from heat as this will merely start the bacteria quickly multiplying again. Rinse washed dishes in water with a dash of household bleach, dry them and put them away.

Water Purification:

■ Before starting the trip, get lessons from a pharmacist on how to purify water, work filters and use flocculents correctly.

■ Test to see how much water a single filtering device can produce (you may need a couple to supply a large group reasonably quickly).

■ Take plenty of spares as hand pumping too forcefully can damage the filter, while very muddy water will quickly clog it.

Tips on avoidance and treatment

For wilderness leaders, training in medical preparedness is essential. Rather than inducing fear, such training instils confidence and a greater sense of responsibility. Developing your hazard awareness will reduce accidents but emergencies may have to be faced anyway. Outside of drowning, cardiac arrest, and serious bleeding (dealt with earlier), here are some very typical river situations, with the appropriate action to be taken.

Medical conditions

Shoulder dislocation

Agonizing when it happens the first time, a dislocated shoulder can sometimes be put back into place in the field by a first aid expert.

To provide relief while the shoulder is still dislocated, keep the arm high and the elbow forward. This is done by strapping a couple of lifejackets between the torso and the arm.

Relaxing the shoulder muscles is the key to reseating the ball in the socket, but it is difficult and extremely painful. The patient will be unable to use the arm and must be taken to medical care.

Hypothermia

Symptoms of mild hypothermia, (cooling of the body core) are shivering and withdrawal. Get the person into warm clothing and shelter. More severe life-threatening cases cause confusion and collapse. One or two other people should get under warm coverings with the patient, communicating continually, and warm him/her up. Give warm drinks such as hot choco-late, but no coffee, tea or alcohol as they stimulate or depress the nervous system. Don't place the patient in front of a fire; this leaves the back of the body exposed and draws circulation away from vital organs. Get a hypothermic patient to hospital.

Medical and emergency checklists

First aid kit: This self-contained kit should be kept in a white box with a red cross. Check usage and replenish items after every trip. Paste a list of items inside the lid of the first aid box.

Basic items
- Floatable waterproof first aid box
- First aid manual and pocket-sized CPR procedure card
- Penlight and torch batteries
- Disposable surgical (latex) gloves
- Sterile plastic water bottles
- Thermometer
- Rubber bands and/or string
- Pocket knife, scissors, and tweezers
- Razor, nailclippers
- Safety pins, needle, cotton
- Roll of duct tape
- Lighters and firestarter
- Water-purifying tablets

For life-threatening emergencies
- Space blanket
- Extra-light reflective blanket
- Orophangeal airways 2, 3, 4 (to open the throat of a patient) ***
- CPR mouthpiece
- Cervical collars, medium & large
- Sterile vacuum-packed gauze dressings (sizes 3 & 5), trauma pads
- Bandages (75mm and 100mm)
- Several packets of gauze swabs
- Cotton wool rolls
- Collapsible splints
- Triangular bandages
- Snakebite kit *
- Syringe pack with adrenaline ***

For routine medical ailments
- Antacid tablets
- Anti-diarrhoea pills
- Anti-nausea pills
- Strong analgesics (painkillers)
- Salt and magnesium tablets (cramps)
- Wide-spectrum antibiotic pills in complete courses **
- Extra rolls of swabs and dressings
- Butterfly plasters (to close wounds)
- Steristrips (for small cuts)
- Sutures **
- Drying ointment (iodine or methyalate)
- Antibiotic ointment **
- Saline drip kit **
- Antibacterial soap
- Ear drops and eye drops
- Eyecup, eyewash and eye patch
- Tampons

> **Note:** * See Medical Tips regarding snakebite.
> ** These items usually need a prescription from a medical doctor. In the case of multiday trips, they should be carried for the group.
> *** Providing drugs or carrying out invasive therapy (cutting, drips or stitching) can be construed as assault in legal terms and should be performed by a medical or paramedical professional.

Emergency kit: This self-contained kit should be in a red box marked 'Emergency'. Do not open it except in cases of emergency. Paste a list of the contents inside the lid.
- Emergency and survival manual
- Cash notes and coins
- Cellular phone with spare battery and charger
- GPS (global positioning system) with manual
- Compass and instructional card
- Detailed topographical map of area with tracks and telecommunications points marked
- Waterproof matches (or in sealed container)
- Lighter, matches, firestarter and candles
- Powerful torches (2) and enough batteries
- Signalling mirror (metal)
- Pen and notepad
- Dehydrated food/energy bars
- Water-purifying tablets
- First aid supplies
- Fishing line and fish hooks
- Small saw or wire saw
- Roll of duct tape
- 5 smoke bombs and 10 pencil flares

> **Note:** The river rescue kit, which includes ropes, is part of your emergency kit.

Dehydration, heat exhaustion

People generally do not drink enough during outdoor exertion, and must be encouraged to take fluids. Drinking too much alcohol at night is a cause of dehydration the next day, so limit intake. Pale, clammy skin, heavy perspiration, yellow discoloured urine, and tiredness or weakness show heat exhaustion. The body temperature is about normal but the person will then develop a headache and may vomit. The treatment is removal from the heat source, rest and consuming plenty of fluids such as isotonic sports drinks. Do not give tea, coffee or alcohol.

Heat stroke

This is a life-threatening condition. The body's temperature control system ceases to work and the person does not perspire, causing body temperature to rise which can lead to possible damage to the brain. The skin is hot and red, body temperature is very high, and dizziness may lead to disorientation or complete collapse, with a rapid pulse. The person must be put in the shade, cooled and wetted, given fluids or an intravenous drip by a qualified person, and observed until medical help is reached.

Environmental threats
Rabid animals

Avoid any animal that staggers, looks sick or appears unusually aggressive. Pre-exposure immunization is recommended for expeditions, but vaccination only partially protects and does not prevent rabies; additional treatment is needed if you are bitten. You need to get to a doctor as quickly as possible.

Snakebite

Snakes inhabit riverine bush and water environs. Most snakes are not deadly poisonous; they are shy and will make off if you leave them. Wear long pants and shoes in snake country. Step on top of logs and rocks, not right over them. Always keep still when a snake is in the vicinity. If bitten, stay calm; shock on its own can be fatal. Try to identify the snake but do not chase the snake to kill it. Different types of venom affect the nervous system, circulation, breathing and body tissue, and require different treatment. Only a qualified person should attempt to administer snakebite serums, which can kill. It is wise to wrap the limb fully with stretch bandage to reduce circulation. Do not use tourniquets. Snakebite victims must be taken to medical care immediately.

Lightning

The 'flash-to-bang' method of measuring the distance of lightning gives a time delay of 1.6km (1 mile) for 5 seconds' time. For lightning at a count of 15 seconds (5km or 3 miles) get down low on land and off the river, away from isolated trees, rock piles or open spaces. Stay away from open shelters. Remove paddles and metal objects and sit out the storm under a tarpaulin, in a deep cave or thick forest.

Diseases

Giardia, cryptospordia and bilharzia are chronic illnesses caused by parasites in the water. Any person with giardia can transmit it by touch and should not handle food. All catering must be very hygienic in giardia areas. Bilharzia is difficult to avoid in endemic areas, but where possible, towel off the skin quickly after exposure to stagnant water or any water suspected to carry the spores.

The best way to avoid malaria (mosquitoes) and oncocerciasis, or river blindness (blackfly), is by not getting bitten. Use insect repellents, stay fully clothed, and remain away from areas of infestation. In malarial areas, cover up in the evenings and sleep under netting. Prophylactic pills are available but take medical advice on this, as well as the correct preparations and dosage for the area you are entering.

Safe and tasty meals

Good meals are as important on a trip as good rapids. Apart from their nutritional value, after a day's exposure to harsh river conditions, a well-presented and tasty meal does wonders for morale.

Rafting parties can carry everything for catering so there should be no excuse for miserable meals. Great 'bush nosh' requires careful planning, packing, hygiene and some imagination.

Planning

■ Appoint a catering manager to plan the menus, buy the food, have the frozen meals prepared, and get the perishables vacuum-packed.

■ Plan meals to include a balance of proteins, carbohydrates and vitamins, with large breakfasts, light lunches and filling dinners. Fruit juices, warm beverages or soups should be served during the day, with the choice depending on the climate. Snacks are good before dinner, while drinking water, tea and coffee should be set out at all times in camp.

■ Ascertain who is vegetarian or has personal or religious food requirements, and plan for them.

■ Assign rotating mealtime duties for food preparation, clean-up and repacking. Caution everyone about hygiene.

■ An upturned raft can make a good table for snacks but do not use for meals because hot food and cutlery may possibly damage the fabric.

Packing

■ As a general rule, pack a day's provisions in a single dry box and label all the boxes per day. List the box contents and the menus inside the lid.

■ Ice cream and frozen foods can be carried for as long as a week even in a hot climate. Freeze in 'tupperware' plastic containers and transfer to dry boxes lined with newspaper. Place blocks of dry ice in plastic over the load and seal the box with duct tape.

■ Blocks of ice will also last many days in seldom-opened boxes. Ensure the ice was made with sterile water. Don't allow food to swill around in melted ice.

■ Fruit and vegetables should be carried under sterile conditions in sealed boxes. Fresh milk tends to go off even when kept cool, so take longlife milk.

Hygiene

■ Bacteria spread rapidly in the warm and wet environment of rivers. Food handlers must wash their hands in disinfectant and wear clean clothes. No one who is ill, especially with a gastrointestinal complaint, should prepare or serve food.

■ Pack enough drinking cups, plates and cutlery for every individual to have a complete set at each meal.

■ Discard potentially hazardous food (e.g. punctured cans, day-old salads).

■ Cutting boards should be cleaned with disinfectants and only impervious plastic used. Cooking utensils should be made of stainless steel, aluminium, glass or cast iron.

■ Wash dishcloths in boiled and bleached water. Burn all burnable items in the fire pan. Keep the dry boxes sanitary to avoid bacteria.

Imagination

River meals should ideally be fresh and natural. Masses of good ideas for imaginative outdoor menu planning are to be found on the Internet and in book-stores.

■ People love variety but also crave traditional staples like buttery bread and barbecued meat.

■ Some planners give an ethnic flavour to each day's menus or vary the style with 'hobo' meals (dipped bread, campfire chilli or fish on a stick). Whatever the theme, ensure the food is colourful and looks good when served.

NOURISHING MEALS LIKE THIS HEARTY STEW, ALWAYS GO DOWN WELL AFTER A LONG TIRING DAY ON THE RIVER.

Glossary

Belay To pass a rope around the body, a rock or a tree, or through a belaying loop called an anchor, in order to brake it with friction.

Big water Large-volume rapids.

Boil Water 'boils' up to the surface due to unevenness of the riverbed or subsurface turbulence.

Boulder Large rocks sticking up out of the river may be widely dispersed (a 'boulder garden') or tightly clustered (a 'boulder sieve').

Carabiner, 'biner or 'crab' A clip used for quick attachment of ropes to anchors, rope to rope or solidly attaching gear or any object.

Cfs / cumecs Cubic feet per cubic metres or seconds, measures of water volume flowing past a single point.

Chute A fast sluice formed when the river is forced through a narrow passage.

Cushion (or pillow) Current flowing around an obstruction such as a branch or rock creates a hump-backed cushion.

Eddy The reversal of the current behind an obstacle.

Eddy fence or eddy line The interface or shear between the upsteam and downstream flow of currents.

Ferry, ferry glide Moving the boat against the river at an angle, either facing upstream (forward ferry) or down-stream (back or reverse ferry), using the current to push it sideways.

Grade/Class A term to describe the international rating of rapids on a scale of 1 – 6 (ascending in difficulty or danger).

Hole or hydraulic Where moving water pours over a sudden drop and flows to the bottom, aerated water flows back upstream to fill the depression: this is the hole.

Lateral A raised current or wave that sets at an angle and is not directly across the main flow.

Line A planned or chosen route through a rapid or section of river.

PFD Personal flotation device. It is worn to assist swimmers and protects the body from impact.

Pinning Entrapment in a boat against obstacles like rocks, trees or pylons.

Pivot or spin A quick turn of the raft on its axis.

Portage Term for carrying a boat around an unrunnable section or between bodies of water.

Pourover Water flowing over a rock or boulder to form a hole on the other side.

Raftmaster The skipper or oarsman leading the crew on a river trip.

Run Describes a section of river. A run also describes the act of actually paddling down the river.

Scout The act of examining a rapid or particular run before running it.

Self-bailing A self-bailing raft allows excess water out of the boat automatically.

Shuttle Using vehicles (or any other transport) to move people and gear between put-in and take-out points.

Siphon A dangerous phenomenon where the current passes through submerged tunnels and spews out elsewhere.

Sneak Taking an easier, more conservative or less dangerous route or line through a rapid.

Strainer Any dangerous obstacle in the water that allows water but not larger solid objects to pass freely.

Sweep Boat The trailing or last boat in an organized river running group.

Sweeper An obstacle like a branch which hangs low over moving water.

Throwbag A bag that holds a long rope stuffed into it; the rope peels out when the bag is thrown.

Throwline A coiled line used for throwing in preference to a throwbag.

Tracking The inherent capability of a water-borne craft to stay in a straight line and hold that course.

Undercut An overhanging rock, ledge or cave below the surface of the current flow.

Vector A force applied at an angle to a tensioned line to increase the tension or haul.

Weir Low-head dam, forming a symmetrical suck-back that can be fatal.

Wrap When a boat is wrapped around an obstacle by the forces of the current on its opposite ends.

Z-Drag or Z-Pulley A 3:1 mechanical advantage rope haul system.

KEY TO WHITEWATER CONTACTS FOR RIVERS

■ Name ■ Web address ■ E-mail address ■ Mailing address ■ Tel. country/regional code ■ Tel. number

Rafting Associations

■ **American Whitewater**
■ www.awa.org ■ info@awa.org ■ 1430 Fenwick Lane, Silver Spring, MD 20910 USA
■ 1 301   589-9453

■ **Australian Canoe Union**
■ www.canoe.org.au ■ auscanoe@canoe.org.au
■ PO Box 666, Glebe, NSW, 2037 Australia
■ 61 2 ■ 9552 4500; 9552 4457

■ **British Canoe Union**
■ www.bcu.org.uk ■ info@bcu.org.uk ■ Adbolton Lane, West Bridgford, Nottingham, NG2 5AS UK
■ 44 1159 ■ 9821100

■ **Canadian Rivers Council**
■ rafting@cyberus.ca ■ CP 212 ■ Bryson, Quebec, JOX 1HO Canada ■ 1 819 ■ 647-3625; 647-6760

■ **German Canoe Federation**
■ www.kanu.de ■ service@kanu.de ■ PO Box 100315, Duisburg, 47003 Germany
■ 49 203 ■ 997-590; 997-5960

■ **International Rafting Federation**
■ Federation of numerous national rafting associations
■ www.IntRaftFed.com/
■ thansen@iafrica.com ■ PO Box 18634, Wynberg, 7800 Cape Town, South Africa ■ 27 21 ■ 761-9298

■ **New Zealand Rafting Association**
■ rangitatarafts@xtra.co.nz ■ PO Box 3859, Christchurch,New Zealand ■ 64 3 ■ 374-3735; 374-5983

■ **Scottish Rafting Association** ■ www.rafting.co.uk
■ splashraft@compuserve.com ■ Dunkeld Road, Aberfeldy, Perthshire PH15 2AQ ■ 44 1887 ■ 829706

Transnational tour operators

■ **Adrift**
■ www.adrift.co.nz ■ raft@adrift.co.nz ■ PO Box 310, Queenstown, New Zealand ■ 64 3 ■ 442-5458; 442-5950

■ **Bio Bio Expeditions Worldwide**
■ www.bbxrafting.com
■ H2OMarc@aol.com OR LarsAlvarez@compuserve.com
■ PO Box 2028, Truckee, CA 96160 California, USA
■ 1 530 ■ 582-6865

■ **Boojum Expeditions**
■ www.boojumx.com ■ webinfo@boojum.com
■ 14543 Kelly Canyon Road ■ Bozeman ■ MT 59715
■ Montana, USA ■ 1 406 ■ 587-0125

■ **Destination Wilderness**
■ www.wildernesstrips.com ■ destwild@bendnet.com
■ PO Box 1965, Sisters OR 97759 Oregon, USA
■ 1 541 ■ 549-1336

■ **Earth River**
■ www.earthriver.com ■ earthriv@ulster.net
■ 180 Towpath Rd, Accord, New York, NY 12404 USA
■ 1 914 ■ 626-2665

■ **Mountain Travel Sobek**
■ www.mtsobek.com ■ info@mtsobek.com
■ 6420 Fairmount Ave, El Cirrito, 94530, California, USA
■ 1 510 ■ 527-8100

■ **Project Raft**
■ www.raft.org/indexo.html ■ project@raftweb
■ Project Whitewater ■ 2915 Brittan Avenue San Carlos, California CA 94070-3520 USA ■ 1 650
■ 508-8811

■ **Baikal Rafting**
■ www.icc.ru/baikalcomplex ■ travel@irk.ru ■ PO Box 3598, Irkutsk-29, Russia ■ 7 3952 ■ 35-9205; 46-4762; 43-2060

Index

Photographic credits

Anders Blomqvist: p 86; **Andrew Kellett:** p 35; **ARK:** pp 19 (C, D, E, G: bottom left), 23 (B), 65 (B, C); **Bill Hatcher Photography:** pp 8 (top left), 13, 33, 44 (bottom left & right), 53, 62; **Christian Kallen:** p 82; **Damian Krige:** p 65 (E); **David Rogers:** p 19 (G: bottom right); **David Wall:** pp 9, 78 (top left); **Dugald Bremner Studio:** pp 41, 42, 46; **Felix Unite:** p 59 (bottom left); **Gallo Images/Brian Bailey:** p 14; **Gallo Images/Steve Bly:** p 11 (bottom right); **Gallo Images/Dugald Bremner:** p 18; **Graeme Addison:** pp 28 (bottom left), 36, 37 (E), 55, 58, 67 (bottom), 70 (top), 71 (bottom), 72; **Holger Leue:** p 17; **Ian Trafford:** pp 2, 5, 6, 22, 40 (top left), 63, 75, 79, 89; **INPRA/Tony Berle:** p 24 ; **INPRA/Sygma/Luc-Henri Fage:** p 48; **Justin Fox:** pp 12, 23 (C, D), 37 (A, B, D), 38, 45, 65 (A, D), 88 (top left); **Kumsheen Adventures:** p 29; **Mary Duncan:** pp 16, 25; **Mountain Camera/John Cleare:** pp 10 (top left), 83; **New Holland Australia/Shaen Adey:** p 80; **Photo Access Library/ James Kay:** cover; **Photo Access Library/Tim Barnett:** p 10 (top right); **Photo Access Library:** p 15; **Prijon:** pp 19 (A, F, H), 23 (A), 37 (C); **Struik Image Library/Anthony Johnson:** pp 19 (B), 39, 93; **Zambezi Promotions:** p 84.

Publisher's acknowledgements: The publishers would like to thank Fallright International Rescue, Extreme Adventures, ARK Rafts and Cape Union Mart for their assistance in providing equipment for photo shoots.